HIDDEN HISTORY
of
PINEHURST

Julia Hans

THE
History
PRESS

Published by The History Press
Charleston, SC
www.historypress.com

Front cover: Several LPGA founders in front of the Pinehurst Country Club. *Tufts Archives*.
Back cover: Pinehurst caddies line up. *Tufts Archives*.

First published 2024

Manufactured in the United States

ISBN 9781467156257

Library of Congress Control Number: 2023950479

To my sister, Nancy Hoffman

CONTENTS

ACKNOWLEDGEMENTS

While writing a book seems like a solitary endeavor, many people contribute to the overall project. First, I'd like to thank Sandy Gernhart for helping me navigate the deep waters of the Tufts Archives. Sandy was instrumental in steering me toward valuable documents and knowledgeable people, especially while researching the Sandhills Woman's Exchange. She fielded all my questions and reviewed an early draft of chapter 3. This project would have floundered without her help. I also thank Meriwether Cowgill Schmid and Susan Taylor-Schran for generously sharing their knowledge with me about the Exchange.

The folks at the Moore County Historical Association were generous with their time and resources, providing photographs and giving me a private tour of the Shaw House. I especially thank Susan Pockmire for helping with the pictures. I'm indebted to Audrey Moriarty at the Given Memorial Library for sharing her groundbreaking research on the women of Pinehurst. I also thank Dr. Gwynn Thayer of the North Carolina State University Libraries and chief curator for their Special Collections Research Center, who generously shared her compilation of the caddie scrapbook. I am grateful to Nadine Moody of the Taylortown Museum for sharing her expertise on the history of African Americans in the Pinehurst area.

For one week in July 2023, I was a writer-in-residence at the magnificent Weymouth Center for the Arts and Humanities in Southern Pines, North Carolina. In the quiet and solitude, I made tremendous strides on the manuscript. I thank the kind staff at the center for making me feel so welcome, particularly Katie Wyatt, executive director, and Holmes Hall, director of property management. What a special place.

Procuring more than eighty rare, historic photographs for this book was difficult, especially since many are no longer available to the public, free of charge. I had to turn to institutions in the state or use material in the public domain. As such, I am grateful to Jason E. Tomberlin, head of research and instructional services at the Wilson Special Collections Library, University of North Carolina–Chapel Hill. Jason worked wonders in obtaining dozens of historical photos and postcards for me. Scholars must have free and open access to material culture, and I appreciate all that the staff at the Wilson Library does to make this possible.

I thank Kate Jenkins at The History Press for being an erudite editor and patiently fielding all my questions and concerns. It is a joy to work with such an editor. I thank my husband, Ravi Hans, and my children, Michael Hans, Kristin Stevens, and Abigail Nickols, for their continued interest in my work. Finally, I thank my big sister, Nancy Hoffman, to whom this book is dedicated. Throughout my life, Nancy has been my mentor, ally, cheerleader, and partner in crime. We have been friends since childhood and now, into our dotage. I am blessed to have a sister-friend like you.

INTRODUCTION

My son and daughter-in-law brought me to Pinehurst three years ago to get coffee and walk around the village center. As we strolled along the sandy sidewalks, past the old cottages and historic hotels, under magnolia trees the size of maples, I kept wondering—have I been here before? Why does this look so familiar? But I had never set foot in Pinehurst or seen the town in a televised golf tournament. As a kid, if a golf tournament came on during the Wide World of Sports, I would change the channel faster than Usain Bolt off the starting blocks. The first time I heard someone mention "Pinehurst No. 2," I thought it was a coffee shop. I swear on Dave Barry's soul, I'm not making that up. Why, then, did the village seem so familiar?

Fast-forward a few years, and I live in Moore County. While exploring the area, I stumbled upon the Tufts Archives in the Given Memorial Library, which is like finding hidden treasure for an academic like me. As I delved into the archives, I learned that Pinehurst was designed to look like a traditional New England town. And that's when it clicked. For this native New Englander, the curvy roads, small clapboard cottages, and village green (we'd call it the "town common") looked like home. When a friend from up North came to visit, the first thing she said about Pinehurst village was, "This looks just like Concord." She meant Concord, Massachusetts, home of the shot heard 'round the world in 1775.

As I was tooling through the archives, the writer in me saw the potential for several books. Initially, I wanted to write about the women of Pinehurst, like Gertrude Tufts, Annie Oakley, and the movers and shakers of the Sandhills

Woman's Exchange. But when the Hidden History series came into view, I realized this would be a better choice, giving me the freedom to write on broader subjects.

But why write a book about Pinehurst when several have already been written? While there are books about the town's history, they focus on golf, golfers and golf courses written by, you guessed it, golfers. Further, books like *The Spirit of Pinehurst* and *Pinehurst Stories* were published by Pinehurst, Inc., while others were published by sports or tourism industries. As such, these books, while containing pertinent information, serve more as marketing tools than detached historical records.

From its beginning, Pinehurst writers have not exactly been objective. The local newspaper, the *Pinehurst Outlook*, which started in 1897, was owned by the Tufts family and produced by the village. The paper announced sporting events and social happenings, but it often reads like a marketing brochure. Articles from the *Outlook* are rife with hyperbole, as in this article from March 24, 1906:

> *Pinehurst is, to be brief, the most complete and perfectly equipped Fall, Winter and Spring Resort in the world.…Possessing exceptional opportunities for outdoor life, it also offers right conditions for living in every sense of the word; its unsurpassed location in the far famed long-leaf pine thermal belt or Sand Hill region, responsible for a winter climate generally acknowledged to possess few equals in the rare purity of its air, and the subtle tonic of its sunshine.*

And that is from a news article! Here's another from 1904:

> *The air is dry and purified by the pine forests which give off ozone as freely as any vegetation. There is a constant light breeze, which gives freshness and is exhilarating and stimulating. The water is a natural mineral water, and is recommended for those suffering with gastric and intestinal digestive disturbances.… "Good for kidney and bladder problems" salts in the water are "of great value to infants and children for their bone forming properties."*

According to the *Outlook*, the Pinehurst air would cure all sicknesses, and the water would produce a new generation of *wunderkinds*. Given the lack of objective historical narratives, then, it was time for a town history to be written by an outsider with no stakes in the game.

In writing *Hidden History of Pinehurst*, I wasn't looking for salacious stories but narratives that have been ignored or sidelined. I also wanted to give the reader a sense of time and place, which meant delving into uncomfortable historical narratives. What was it like for African Americans who worked in Pinehurst but could not live within village limits? What was it like for the caddies to live under Jim Crow laws? The *Outlook* provided ample material to build a backdrop. In its pages, I read about cakewalks and beautiful baby contests, about the "colored mammy" used by the Woman's Exchange and about the myth of the "happy caddy." Writing about Pinehurst meant writing about the racially charged South and the Black people who built the village and golf courses, something local writers often sidestepped. Some books on Pinehurst never mention African Americans, and I did not want to participate in that sort of narrative erasure.

During my research, I encountered people disinclined to discuss Pinehurst's racial past. When I interviewed someone about their recollections, they avoided answering my questions about the African Americans who built the golf courses. Another interviewee talked haltingly about racism during the 1940s and suggested I keep such "negatives" out of my book. I don't see it that way. My job as a writer and historian is not to produce an airbrushed marketing tool but an account of the town's history from as many perspectives as possible. My book does not tackle the complexities of racial dynamics in the South—a task too big for my skills—but I do include some description of what life in the village might have been like for African Americans who helped build Pinehurst. And that leads me to the contents of this book.

Every history book has its parameters, and *Hidden History of Pinehurst* covers the village's first fifty years (except for the chapter on the Woman's Exchange). While many know Pinehurst as "the cradle of American golf," I felt that few appreciate the village's origin story. James Walker Tufts founded Pinehurst with people of modest means in mind who were in poor health or who just wanted to escape the harsh New England winters. Golf was the furthest thing from his mind. In chapter 1, I focus on Tufts's philanthropic and progressive vision and how it was influenced by his friend Edward Everett Hale and the Lend-a-Hand Society.

In chapter 2, I profile some of Pinehurst's best-known caddies. If you've ever seen historic photographs of Pinehurst's golf courses, you will notice two outstanding characteristics: sand greens and African American caddies. Pinehurst's caddies grew into the stuff of legend because their knowledge of the courses, especially the difficult No. 2, could win golfers tournaments. However, the rise of the Pinehurst caddie coincided with racial segregation and the harsh effects of Jim Crow laws.

In chapter 3, I tell the history of the Sandhills Woman's Exchange. When I started my research, I asked one of the librarians, "Where is the material on the women who built Pinehurst?" She looked at me blankly and said, "The women didn't build Pinehurst. The men did." Sure, women may not have financed the village or designed the buildings and golf courses, but women played a significant role in shaping Pinehurst. Enter the Sandhills Woman's Exchange, part of a nationwide benevolent society. Since 1922, the Exchange has helped rural women earn money through the consignment of goods. Devoted volunteers kept the Exchange afloat despite the Great Depression, two world wars, and near bankruptcy; its mission continues today.

Chapter 4 focuses on Annie Oakley's years in Pinehurst. While I knew Oakley was a sharpshooter who had performed with Buffalo Bill's Wild West, I did not know about her philanthropy or her years in Pinehurst. Oakley and her husband, Frank Butler, spent seven winters in Pinehurst after they retired. During that time, Oakley gave numerous exhibitions for charity and free shooting lessons to women. Oakley was a lifelong advocate for women using firearms, and she believed that Pinehurst's "idle women" (her words) would be better off knowing how to defend themselves.

Of course, no book about Pinehurst would be complete without a chapter on golfers. While oceans of ink have been spilled writing about men golfers, I wanted to take a different tack. In chapter 5, I highlight nine pioneers of women's golf, athletes who won the Women's Amateur North and South Tournament, an event held in Pinehurst since 1903 (the men's, since 1901). Several of the women profiled in this chapter were founders of the Ladies Professional Golf Association (LPGA). The cover photograph captures some of these women in front of the iconic Pinehurst Country Club.

With more than forty golf courses in Moore County, it's hard to imagine a time when folks did anything else. But in prewar days, villagers got up to some zany antics. Not only would they dress up for costume balls and dance the night away at the Carolina Ballroom, but they also liked to race greased pigs, play donkey polo, and try their hand at jalopy soccer. They watched polo games at the Harness Racetrack and moseyed down to the gun club for shooting or archery lessons. If you were part of the Tin Whistles, you might be invited back to Mr. Barber's digs to play miniature golf. The final chapter takes a lighthearted look at some of Pinehurst's other outdoor sports.

Ultimately, I hope these lesser-known narratives—stories about women, philanthropists, and African Americans—round out the history of Pinehurst.

Chapter 1

PINEHURST, 1 B.G. (BEFORE GOLF)

Golf was not even a remote consideration in the initial vision of Pinehurst.
—*Chris Buie,* The Early Days of Pinehurst

A YANKEE VILLAGE IN THE HEALTH-GIVING PINES

People often assume that Pinehurst was founded for the Vanderbilt set, who summered in Newport and wintered in Florida with a stopover in the Sandhills for a round of golf. But founder James Walker Tufts had neither the wealthy class nor the game of golf in mind when he conceived his village. The Boston businessman, who made his fortune with the American Soda Fountain Company, sold his shares when he was sixty and purchased about six thousand acres of sandy, clear-cut land in the Sandhills of North Carolina. He intended to build a health resort for people of modest means.

Why there? At the turn of the century, it was believed that pine forest air had curative properties. Tufts, who himself was unwell (some accounts say it was early-stage tuberculosis), often traveled south for the winter. According to his grandson Richard S. Tufts, James Walker's health improved dramatically after wintering in the South. Tufts had also heard near-miraculous reports of the Sandhills' healing properties. His friend Reverend Benjamin Goodridge of Dorchester told James Walker that his wife had made a spectacular recovery after spending a season in Southern Pines. Further, Tufts read in the *Encyclopedia Britannica* that the climate in Moore County was like Italy and France, where tuberculosis was virtually unknown. He conferred with

Above: Early Pinehurst
Village showing sand
roads. *Moore County
Historical Association.*

Right: James Walker Tufts.
*Moore County Historical
Association.*

Opposite: Main Street
early days. *Moore County
Historical Association.*

VIEW AT PINEHURST, N.C.

This is the main street in Pinehurst. Jeanne Push

researchers at North Carolina State University in Raleigh, who assured him that the Sandhills had a healthy climate and that the mild falls and winters had low humidity. From personal experience to firsthand testimonies to scientific research, Tufts was convinced that the Sandhills would be the perfect place for his health resort. And so, in 1895, Tufts made his first down payment on about 500 acres. A year later, he purchased 5,980 acres for $7,400, most of it from the Page family. The plans for his village were underway.

The locals thought he was crazy, calling his village "Tuft's Folly." Everyone knew that the longleaf pines were the only valuable resource in the area, but these had been exploited for sap, turpentine, and cut lumber. As for farming, nothing grew in the sandy soil. (The area wasn't called the "Pine Barrens" for nothing.) Tufts was undeterred. The village would be funded by his substantial fortune and, he hoped, by the sale of peaches, which grew in abundance. He claimed that the village would be a "semi-philanthropic venture" where people in poor health might come to rest and recuperate, yet it would be founded on sound business practices.

Tufts had early-stage tuberculosis patients in mind when he first conceived Pinehurst. However, before the paint was dry on the Holly Inn, it was learned that consumption was highly contagious in all its stages, not just in the final stage, as previously believed. And so, like a savvy businessman, he knew when to pivot. Pinehurst would now become a winter haven where those suffering from respiratory and lung problems could be restored to health by breathing the pine-filled air. (At the same time, the peach crop that Tufts believed would finance his health resort was decimated by the San Jose scale, a perfidious pest. The orchards would never recover.) Tufts would stress that Pinehurst was a "health resort for the weary and overworked, not a sanitarium." Here's James Walker writing about his village:

> *It* [Pinehurst] *is not intended to be a sanitarium for hopeless invalids. It has no hospital features. It is a bright, cheery village, artistically laid out. Possessed of all modern comforts and conveniences, carefully controlled so as to make its sanitary conditions permanent. It invites those in whom disease has not progressed so far as to render recovery impossible. To such, whether of large or small means, it offers advantages absolutely unequalled.*

Tufts wanted the village to be affordable for people of modest means, and he built his cottages and boardinghouses accordingly. Most of the original cottages were simple clapboard structures with one or two bedrooms. Tufts even subsidized transportation, arranging for reduced railroad fares from New England to Southern Pines. Tufts described Pinehurst as "an ideal home for people of small means who need rest and recuperation in a mild climate."

Tufts wanted his village to be modeled after a traditional New England town, so he hired the preeminent Boston firm Olmsted, Olmsted, and Eliot to design his town. Their plan included a village green at the center surrounded by curvilinear roads. (The curvy roads were chosen because they were in vogue at the time and because Olmsted believed they followed the land's natural contour better than a grid pattern might.) As in most New England towns, the village green was the focal point. However, they had trouble growing grass in Pinehurst, so Tufts had winter rye planted the first year. Eventually, the village green gave way to a pine grove. To complete the picture, Tufts hired a New England physician to tend to the village's sick folk, a New England schoolteacher to educate the children, and a New England minister to preach the sermons. To stir up business, Tufts sent letters and booklets to physicians in Boston trumpeting the healing properties of what he called his "Yankee village in the health-giving pines." Capitalizing on the national outdoor fitness craze, Tufts also advertised his village as an ideal place for outdoor sports and recreation like hunting, riding, shooting, and tennis. It wasn't until 1897, when some of his visitors were hitting small white balls in his pastures, disturbing his prized cows, that Tufts thought of adding golf to his list of outdoor activities.

Schooner used to transport goods. *Moore County Historical Association.*

The plan for the village was drawn up on July 6, 1895, and the first guests arrived a mere six months later, on December 31, 1895. Within that time, a dozen or so cottages and a boardinghouse, along with the Holly Inn, were erected. The General Office Building (also called the "Casino") and department store were completed a year later. The Boston firm of Taylor, Kendall, and Stevens were the architects. An estimated 450 workers—Black and white—were hired to clear land, erect buildings, and work on infrastructure, including building roads, installing a trolley line to Southern Pines, and building a power plant.

Pinehurst was a seasonal village at the onset: the electricity was turned on November 1 and switched off on May 15. Few original cottages had kitchens, so tenants could buy their meals at the nearby Casino: three daily meals for $4.50 per week. Hotels like the Magnolia Inn also served food, advertising "northern cooks serving simple Yankee meals" to appeal to northern guests.

While most people think of a casino as a place to gamble, the Casino in Pinehurst, built in 1896, was a common civic building. The first floor contained a large dining room, a ladies' parlor, a café, and a bakery. The second floor housed the men's smoking room, a billiards game room, and a barbershop. In 1899, a bowling alley was added in the back. Situated nearby, the department store, built in 1896, is a two-story wood frame structure that looks much the same today. Constructed with North Carolina pine shingles,

Holly Inn with trolley in front. *Wilson Special Collections Library, UNC–Chapel Hill.*

the first floor housed the store, while the second floor had some apartments (known as the "Franklin Flats") and offices. Inventories from the turn of the century are packed with a dizzying array of goods from groceries and dry goods to furniture and clothing. One could buy dog brushes, Yankee soap, macaroni, axle grease, vinegar, syrup, salt, bicycles, stationery, fire extinguishers, canned lobster, and headache drops, to name just a few items. No wonder their slogan was "We have it, or will get it." The store boasted a delivery service, a Western Union office, and a telephone service where villagers could place local or long-distance calls.

Farming was also part of Pinehurst's attractions. Within the first year of operation, Tufts built poultry and dairy farms, a piggery and about twenty acres dedicated to market gardens, which grew produce for human and animal consumption. The dairy farm stretched to over one hundred acres, and the poultry farm was the largest in the state. The farms were open to the public, so guests could stop by and watch cows being milked, chicks being hatched, and crops being harvested. The Pinehurst farms were free range, so farm animals, razorback hogs, and other wildlife would sometimes sneak into the village, especially if one of the gates was left open. That necessitated building a seven-foot fence around the village's perimeter. Woe to the person who left one of the gates open: there was a stiff fifty-dollar fine for such an infraction. (The fence was taken down in

1910.) Firsthand accounts tell us that some cottages were initially built on posts and that razorback hogs liked to get under the houses to scratch their backs, much to the dismay of the homeowners.

A few miles south of the village green stood an enclosed park for a herd of tame deer. Each year, villagers participated in a deer-naming contest. One favorite, a large buck, was dubbed "Sears Roebuck." According to one record, a man visited the deer park to see the tame herd. When a large buck came up to greet him, the man reached out to shake his antlers. The man got the shock of his life when the deer's antlers came off in his hand.

Perhaps one of the marvels of the village was how quickly Tufts managed to build an infrastructure. Food and supplies for Pinehurst would arrive at the train depot in Southern Pines, and Tufts had to find a way to transport these goods to his village.

The main thoroughfare between the two towns, now Midland Road, was a dusty, bumpy pathway difficult to traverse. Sturdy horse-drawn wagons called "schooners" were used to transport goods down Midland Road. People were transported from the depot in Southern Pines to the Holly Inn in Pinehurst via horse-drawn trolleys. Tufts eventually had an electric trolley system built between Pinehurst and Southern Pines. During the peak season,

Department store. *Moore County Historical Association.*

trolleys would make up to seven daily trips. Electric trolleys were used until around 1907, when the automobile made them obsolete.

A few firsthand accounts by guests have survived. Mrs. Robert Shelander of Sharon, Massachusetts, stayed in the village in 1897, as recommended by her doctor. Mrs. Shelander gives us one of the few glimpses into the Black community on Pinehurst's outskirts. She writes, "After dark, from outside

Opposite and above: Deer park. *Wilson Special Collections Library, UNC–Chapel Hill.*

the fence, we could hear the rich voices of negroes singing, not tunes, but beautiful chords and harmonies." Shelander writes about "colored people with their huts all around" the perimeter of the village. During a raging forest fire that threatened the village, guests took shelter indoors. According to Mrs. Shelander, the "negroes" had waded into the creek and hunkered down under wet blankets to avoid the fire and smoke after first burying the guests' laundry. This, after all, was their livelihood.

Even though he was an ardent abolitionist, James Walker Tufts had to work within the racial hierarchy of time and place. In a letter to his wife, Mary, dated July 16, 1895, Tufts is concerned about accommodating his African American workers. He writes about shanties being constructed to house both Blacks and whites. In the same letter, Tufts writes, "It is strange and pitiful to see how anxious the men are to get work. There were three colored men over on my place yesterday…[who] walked 8 miles just in the hope of getting work from me. Indeed, I am not expected to find even shelter for them."

Tufts seems bothered that he isn't even *expected* to find shelter for the African Americans. A day later, he writes to his wife again about the workforce:

> *We are putting lots of colored and white men to clear the town site and it is getting to be a busy place. Next week…we shall have a number of shanties*

Schooner used to transport goods. *Wilson Special Collections Library, UNC–Chapel Hill.*

Schooner used to transport goods. *Moore County Historical Association.*

Sand pathways, some connecting to Taylortown. *Wilson Special Collections Library, UNC–Chapel Hill.*

> *ready for them to occupy. The darkey town will have to wait I suppose, and as I seem to get all the help clearing that I need I may not build their quarters till later on.... They can sleep under the bushes or on pinestraw.*

It's curious that Tufts says accommodations for African Americans will have to wait, "I suppose," as if resigned to working within the social conventions. The words "they can sleep under the bushes or on pinestraw" sound like an echo of statements made by a white foreman. Tufts seems to be wrestling with social constraints and racist customs. In the building of Pinehurst, a racially mixed workforce was overseen by local white men who

Sand pathways. *Wilson Special Collections Library, UNC–Chapel Hill.*

ensured that African American workers were pushed to the bottom of the labor hierarchy. According to one source, during the building of Pinehurst, African Americans earned about half the wages of their white counterparts. Although local historians have virtually ignored the contribution of Blacks in building Pinehurst, it's clear that the village and golf courses would not have been built without their labor.

CONSTRUCTIVE PHILANTHROPY

By all accounts, Tufts believed in constructive philanthropy and used his fortune to help those in need, particularly his employees in Boston. Now, he was using his earnings to provide affordable housing in his North Carolina town. A vivid picture emerges if we contrast his actions to those of his wealthier, more famous contemporary, George Washington Vanderbilt. Vanderbilt constructed Biltmore House in Asheville, North Carolina— touted as the country's largest private residence—not to help the less fortunate but to display his wealth and power. Vanderbilt opened the Biltmore mansion in 1895, the same year Tufts broke ground in Pinehurst. Later in life, Tufts wrote that he believed there were two kinds of wealthy men: 1) those who used their money to please themselves, thereby widening the gap between economic classes, and 2) those who used their money to help the poor, thereby lessening the gap. Tufts fashioned himself according to the second kind.

How did Tufts develop his humanitarian vision? We know that he was born into a working-class family—his father was a blacksmith, so he certainly could commiserate with the less fortunate. When he was fourteen, Tufts wrote a paper arguing that "the accumulation of wealth carried with it an obligation to share its benefits with those less fortunate." From a young age, Tufts believed in using wealth for altruistic rather than egotistic purposes.

Like many New Englanders, Tufts had deep Puritan roots (that explains the no alcohol or beer policy). He was also profoundly influenced by his contemporary, the Unitarian minister Edward Everett Hale, founder of the Lend-a-Hand Society in Boston. According to Richard Tufts, Edward and James were "warm friends." The two men collaborated closely on this new community in the pines. Hale wrote that Tufts had one vision in mind when he founded Pinehurst: "with an eye single to bettering the condition of his fellow man and affording the northern invalid opportunity for enjoying the benefits of an unexcelled health resort at a moderate expense." Tufts's constructive philanthropy even extended to locals. According to William H. Watt, when Tufts returned from one of his trips to Florida, he told Dr. Hale that "what he had seen had impressed him and expressed a wish to do something to assist in lightening the burdens of the Sandhills farmers."

Hale was the village's most vocal supporter. One of the most influential men in Boston in the late 1800s and great-grandson of the Patriot Nathan Hale, Edward Everett was a revered writer, what we today might call an "influencer." Between his writing and preaching, Hale had an enormous audience. (Hale edited or wrote more than sixty books in various genres, from fiction to biography to travelogues.) He was an abolitionist and advocate for educational and social reform, pushing for Indian rights and the free education of women and Blacks.

In 1886, Hale founded the Lend-a-Hand Society, a charitable organization devoted to helping those in need in Boston. James Walker Tufts was an active member. The organization's motto, written by Hale, reads:

Look up and not down.
Look forward and not back.
Look out and not in.
Lend a hand.

Inspired by the Lend-a-Hand Society, Tufts set up a Mutual Aid Society for his Boston employees and underwrote affordable housing for them, the Bunker Hill Terraces. Tufts also established apprentice schools in Boston and maintained close contact with those he helped. One of Tufts's Boston factory workers wrote, "[Tufts] credited his employees with much of his business success." Writing about Tufts's progressive policies, historian Matthew Taylor Himel notes:

> *Tufts contributed personal funds to the* [North End] *union that established a plumbing school and football team. He also wrote "employee legacies" into his will. Upon his death, each married male employee would receive $200 if they worked at the company for at least two years. Either as a righteous cause or investment in human capital, Tufts's actions went against the typical* Gospel of Wealth *apostle.*

Richard S. Tufts wrote that his grandfather's involvement with the Lend-a-Hand Society "influenced him to start Pinehurst," a detail that seems lost to history.

It's no surprise that when it came time to appoint the first pastor of Pinehurst, Tufts tapped his friend Edward Everett. Tufts even named one of the first cottages built in Pinehurst after his friend ("Hale Cottage"), although evidence suggests Hale never stayed in the cottage. When he was in town, the right reverend preferred to stay at the Holly Inn.

Despite his philanthropic views, Tufts maintained tight control over who would stay in the cottages. One had to be approved by James Walker personally. Guests were required to submit two letters of recommendation before being accepted: one from their physician, attesting to good health, and a second from their minister, attesting to good moral character.

Cakewalks and Baby Contests

Even though Pinehurst was fashioned after a traditional New England village, when it came to entertainment, the town was a product of the Old South. Early editions of the *Pinehurst Outlook* announce card parties, dances and lectures, along with African American beautiful baby contests and cakewalks. Events like the beautiful baby contest and the cakewalk were commonplace throughout the postbellum South, and they took place in Pinehurst from 1899 to around 1921. One headline reads, "Villagers Crowd to See Old-Time Southern Cake Walk." According to the *Outlook*, these annual affairs were wildly popular with villagers.

A March 1, 1901 front-page article in the *Outlook* describes a "colored baby show and cake walk" held in the Village Hall, which drew capacity crowds. The entire front page describes the event. First came the beautiful baby contest, where fifteen babies were assembled on stage, held in the arms of their "proud mammies." The reporter observes that "this was the first opportunity that many of our Northern guests have had to inspect little pickaninnies at short range," as if the babies were an exotic species. A committee of several white women then proceeded to view the contestants: "As the voting proceeded, each lady seeming [*sic*] very anxious that her choice should win. For forty-five minutes, there was a very exciting time, and the front of the stage was a brilliant spectacle of highly animated life."

After much deliberation, the women selected first- and second-place winners, who won $5.00 and $2.50, respectively. Each contestant was also awarded $1.00, with a special $2.00 prize given to sixteen-month-old twins Henry and Dewey.

Between the baby contest and cakewalk were a series of musical and dance acts. First came a male "colored quartette," followed by various singers and dancers. The reporter describes each act in detail and concludes that a trio of singers was the best act of the evening "from a colored standpoint."

Next came the much-anticipated cakewalk, where Black couples danced or promenaded before white judges. The prize winners were given cakes; hence, the name "cakewalk." Historians tell us that the cakewalk, which was first performed by enslaved people in the South, had its roots in African dance and music. Some of the earliest oral histories of formerly enslaved people indicate that these improvisational routines were originally plantation dances, generally taking place on Sundays when the enslaved people might have some time off. Eventually, however, plantation owners got involved and held contests to determine the best performance. The enslaved people were often made to dress in fancy clothing and parade before guests, who served as judges. One social historian writes:

> *Although the exact year and location* [of the cakewalk] *are still undetermined,…the cakewalk was a grand-promenade type of dance, where couples would take turns performing.…The cakewalk was more than a recreational dance; it also gave a chance for enslaved people to ridicule those who tyrannized them. The dancers would dress up in their finest clothes and parodied the mannerisms and dancing of the white Southern elite.*

At the turn of the century, cakewalks performed by African Americans for a white audience were popular in the United States. In 1892, for instance, the Cakewalk Jubilee, a national contest, took place at Madison Square Garden with fifty finalists. Similar events took place in Atlantic City and other major cities. According to Brooke Baldwin, the dance's satiric elements were lost on white audiences. Baldwin argues that the cakewalk's purpose was "to satirize the competing culture of supposedly 'superior' whites." Cakewalks in the postbellum South could be serious and dignified or comic and absurd. Separate competitions were held for children and adults.

In Pinehurst, cakewalks were judged by a group of men, with winning couples awarded cakes provided by the Holly Inn baker. A March 1, 1901 article announces that the cakewalk was a "revelation to a large portion of the audience," which suggests that the audience of northerners had never witnessed a cakewalk before. Perhaps this was part of Pinehurst's take on the "Southern experience" that many northerners came to expect. The reporter describes the event:

> To say that it was a treat is to say very little. It was most amusing and kept the large assemblage in the best possible humor from beginning to end. The grotesque figuring, posturing, and other things incidental to this form of amusement, were all present in pure native simplicity, and the way in which it was received showed how much it was enjoyed by all.

The *Outlook* reported on each cakewalk. A brief article, under the headline "Ethiopian Revels," reads, "The whole entertainment was without any rehearsal and was intended to show the native colored people as they are. The show was universally well-liked and pronounced a complete success." By 1902, however, the annual contest was no longer announced on the front page but was relegated to a few paragraphs deep within the paper. And by 1903, an article in the *Outlook* suggests that interest in the event was waning. However, a standing-room-only crowd indicated otherwise. It seemed that northerners still had an appetite for the cakewalk, for the reporter notes that "keen interest was manifested and applause was liberally bestowed."

According to the *Outlook*, the African American community organized some cakewalks in Pinehurst. Occasionally, a cakewalk was held as a fundraiser. In 1901, for instance, one was held in the village to benefit the "Pickford Sanitarium for colored people." And African Americans might even be hired to participate in a cakewalk and provide musical entertainment after a fox hunt. The annual Pinehurst cakewalk event moved from the Village Hall to the Carolina Hotel. One *Outlook* article from the 1920s reveals that some of the guests at the Carolina Hotel took part in a minstrel show, where they performed songs and did cakewalks while in blackface. By the 1920s, the beautiful baby contests and cakewalks seemed to have died out in the village, as they did throughout the country.

A REFOLIATION MIRACLE

While the firm of Olmsted, Olmsted, and Eliot was hired to draw up plans for the village, their employee, Warren Manning, implemented the design, taking a virtual wasteland and turning it into a verdant, botanical wonder. Olmsted never set foot in Pinehurst.

Manning left the Olmsted firm in December 1895 and began working on the plans for Pinehurst a month later. By then, he had opened his own landscape architectural business in Billerica, Massachusetts. Manning was involved in all the landscape development connected with the village and was consulted until his death in 1938. Manning writes, "I know Mr. Olmstead's personal interest in Pinehurst was a keen one.…While Mr. Olmsted didn't visit Pinehurst personally, he did delegate me to make the visit after the studies were made in the office."

Manning was well suited to overseeing the plans. Son of an accomplished botanist and student of Harvard's famed Arnold Arboretum, Manning was an expert in vegetation. His résumé included designing the grounds of the Biltmore Estate in Ashville, North Carolina; working on exhibits for the Chicago Columbian Exposition of 1893; and implementing park systems in cities such as Milwaukee, Chicago, and Washington, D.C.

When he arrived in Pinehurst in 1896, Manning immediately set up a nursery and ordered more than 200,000 seedlings, with about one-fourth imported from France. His idea was to blend indigenous species like dogwoods, magnolias, and longleaf pine with more exotic plants and trees. He preferred the American style of landscape architecture with its meandering lanes, sprawling design, and natural plant growth. And he had his work cut out for him. The earliest photographs of the village show an area dominated by sandy paths with only an occasional scrawny pine, creating a bleak landscape. Over forty years, he turned a barren wasteland into a verdant paradise, prompting many to call his work a "refoliation miracle." Manning traveled to Pinehurst often and developed a close friendship with Leonard Tufts, which lasted forty years. (Hundreds of personal letters between the two are preserved in the Tufts Archives.)

FROM HEALTH RESORT TO WEALTH RESORT

We know that James Walker Tufts founded Pinehurst as a semi-philanthropic venture for people of modest means. How, then, did Pinehurst become an exclusive golfing destination? The transition occurred more rapidly than one might think, taking place around the time James Walker Tufts departed this earth.

As we recall, it wasn't until 1897, when some of his visitors were hitting small white balls in his pastures, disturbing his prized cows, that Tufts thought of adding golf to his list of leisure activities. In 1898, Tufts commissioned Dr. Leroy Culver of New York to design a nine-hole golf course to protect his cows more than start an industry. This was soon expanded to eighteen holes and was dubbed "Pinehurst No. 1." The clubhouse was built the same year.

In 1900, Tufts hired a Scottish golf course designer named Donald Ross to build a second golf course, Pinehurst No. 2. At the same time, golf was taking off nationally. The United States Golf Association (USGA) was founded in 1894. By the turn of the century, there were nearly one thousand clubs in the United States, all but one located north of Washington, D.C. Many visitors to Pinehurst were northerners who golfed, creating a demand for the sport. All these things—national interest, guests who golfed, and the arrival of Donald Ross—conspired to turn Pinehurst into a golf mecca. (Indeed, Donald Ross would stay connected to the village in one form or another until his death in 1948.)

James Walker Tufts went to his reward in 1902, just seven years after founding Pinehurst. His son Leonard inherited the village, which was on the brink of bankruptcy. Leonard would turn things around economically, making Pinehurst an exclusive golfing destination. And it started with the construction of the Carolina Hotel.

Called the "Queen of the South" or the "White House of Golf" (although the hotel was originally yellow with red shutters), the Carolina Hotel opened its doors on January 1, 1901, catering to wealthy patrons. The Rockefellers, DuPonts, and Morgans all stayed at the Carolina Hotel, where they could play golf in the morning, relax for drinks at the country club in the afternoon,

The Carolina Hotel. *Moore County Historical Association.*

and attend a lavish dinner in formal dress at night. When the focal point of the village changed from the town green to the opulent "Queen of the South," Pinehurst's purpose and clientele changed, too. An *Outlook* article describes how the Carolina was a world unto itself:

> *Two doctors with operating and X-ray equipment, soda fountain, news stand, trained nurse, barber, hairdresser, chiropodist, brokerage office, telegraph and teletype, a men's shop, a shop for ladies, gift shop, photo shop, ball-room dancing instructor, tap-dance teaching, bridge instruction, electrician, carpenter, painter, public stenographer, portrait painter and hostess...by way of diversions, the Carolina offers in the way of recreation: bridge, riding (with one of the finest of riding rings just a few steps from the lobby, where weekly gymkhanas are held), bridge tournaments, keno, ball-room, putting green, archery, entertainers, ping-pong, pool and billiards, putting rugs, checkers, bolo, football novelty, chess, checkers, backgammon, bicycling, indoor quoits...*

And that's only a partial list. Riding parties left the hotel daily. A-list celebrities like Annie Oakley could be found on the front porch, taking women's names for shooting lessons. James Walker Tufts wrote that he hoped the hotel would not create any "distinction in the social and friendly spirit which has thus far been so eminently characteristic of the place." But whether by design or necessity, Leonard Tufts reinvented Pinehurst as a destination for the leisure class, the moneyed traveler who liked the finer things in life. Leonard spent a fortune on rebranding, hiring a New York advertising man, Frank Presbrey, to pitch Pinehurst's new image. Advertisements were placed in magazines like *Town and Country* and *American Golfer*. Historian Matthew Taylor Himel notes that from 1903 to the 1920s, "Presbrey and his agency crafted an image of the village that appealed to affluent Americans from the burgeoning metropolitan cities in the Northeast and Midwest."

Leonard also worked hard to shed the village's reputation as a place for consumptives. Hotel stationery and advertisements from the period emphatically state, "No consumptives accepted." He sold land and some of the cottages but only to a preselected group. He personally had to approve the sale of any lot or any construction plans in the village. Under Leonard's leadership, the Tufts family became increasingly selective about who could stay in their town.

Jim Crow laws mandated racial segregation, relegating Blacks in Pinehurst to out-of-sight workers living in nearby Taylortown. But guest committees also precluded Jewish patrons from renting cottages or staying at hotels. Leonard's assistant, Ethel M. Gray, kept a card file of people who stayed in Pinehurst, and she was careful to cull out any with what she called "suspiciously Hebraic names." In a July 18, 1919 letter to her boss, Gray writes:

> *I was rather drastic on that point, and when doubtful, dropped the prospect, believing that P. [Pinehurst] has reached the place where it can better afford not to solicit a good prospect than give any Hebrew the right to say that Pinehurst has solicited his patronage. So the –steins and –bergs and Weils, Issacs and Solomons are to be passed by.*

Leo approved. Under Leonard's leadership, exclusivity became a selling point, and nothing fosters a sense of exclusivity like a country club.

Pinehurst Country Club members had to pay high fees, and social clubs like the Tin Whistles and the Silver Foils were by invitation only. Writing about the Tin Whistles, Himel notes:

> *The men from Boston, Philadelphia, and New York who organized the Tin Whistles at Pinehurst also acted as "muscle" for the resort. They used their positions as social elites, finance executives, and advertising moguls to promote and present an exclusive community at the resort. They cast doubt on Tufts' hint of philanthropic and Progressive agenda and represented the exclusive nature and local autonomy of Pinehurst.*

Pinehurst Country Club. *Moore County Historical Association.*

What began as a humanitarian effort to help people of modest means had become an enclave for the rich. For better or worse, Tufts's health resort had become a wealth resort.

Under Leonard Tufts's and Donald Ross's leadership, the focus on golf and the golfing lifestyle grew exponentially. By 1919, there were four completed golf courses at Pinehurst, the largest number of courses in the South at the time. By the 1920s, Pinehurst was one of the nation's foremost golfing resorts. One golf historian notes, "It was from Pinehurst that golf rapidly expanded to other sections of American golf," which is why St. Andrews in Hastings, New York, is the "birthplace" of American golf, but Pinehurst is the "cradle." From this small village in the pines, the golfing industry in America would grow and flourish.

Chapter 2

THE CADDIES

The caddie was a very important thing back in the old days of golf and especially at Pinehurst because the greens are so subtle, the breaks, and they knew every little break on those greens. And people listened to those Pinehurst caddies.
—*Patty Kirk Bell*

In the early decades of the twentieth century, Pinehurst's reputation as a premier golf destination grew dramatically. And, just as Pinehurst's courses would become increasingly famous, so, too, would its caddies. Their knowledge of the courses was invaluable to players. Writing to a potential customer, Leonard Tufts assured him that Pinehurst caddies were "first-rate…superior to those at other places." Of course, this may have been part of Tufts's marketing strategy, but there's no doubt that the caddies played a significant role in Pinehurst's golf history. Almost without exception, Pinehurst's caddies were African Americans from Taylortown or West Southern Pines, though occasionally, there might be a "white boy on the course."

The caddie program in Pinehurst was started in 1901 by Donald Ross and three-time PGA champion Paul Runyan. Caddies did more than carry clubs; they also provided insider information about the course's terrain, the roll of the hills, and the way the light hit the greens at a particular time of day. On a notoriously difficult course like Pinehurst No. 2, a good caddie could make the difference between losing or winning a tournament. Even today, it's estimated that about 90 percent of players on No. 2 use caddies.

Young caddies on a trolley. *Tufts Archives.*

During the 1920s, the Pinehurst resort employed more than five hundred caddies ages seven to seventy-five. Twin brothers Herbert and Frank McCaskill worked for the resort when they were twelve, dragging carpets over footprints left behind by golfers on the sand greens. Some photographs show schoolboys carrying golf clubs who could not have been older than six or seven.

The days of the seven-year-old caddie were short-lived, however, for Pinehurst had to abide by North Carolina labor laws. A letter from Donald

Carpet man waiting to clear the sand. Wilson Special Collections Library, UNC–Chapel Hill.

Ross, dated January 19, 1924, reports, "A rep of the N.C. state child welfare commission was in my office yesterday inquiring about the method used at the clubhouse in employing caddies." Ross assured the representative that each child was registered and no one was under sixteen. A year later, Gertrude Tufts, Leonard's wife, was concerned that some of the boys were missing school to caddie. So, she arranged for a bus to take the boys to school and then return them to the club afterward for work.

The rise of the caddie in Pinehurst coincided with enforced racial segregation. Under Jim Crow laws, African Americans were marginalized, denied voting rights, and restricted from many educational and employment opportunities. Historian Lane Demas notes that when Donald Ross was busy designing his Pinehurst courses, North Carolina was in a state of heightened racial tension:

> *Mobs of white Democrats violently retook control of the state government and killed an unknown number of black and white Republicans in Wilmington,*

Pinehurst caddie with golfers on sand green. *Wilson Special Collections Library, UNC–Chapel Hill.*

a significant incident of mass racial violence at the turn of the century. As white supremacists reclaimed North Carolina's government and incidents of lynching and disenfranchisement escalated around the state, black men reclaimed Pinehurst's wastelands, built its courses and maintained the grounds.

While they earned a better income than manual laborers, and while they enjoyed status in their community, caddies still had to endure the humiliation of segregation. This bias pervaded golf institutions throughout the South. For instance, golfer Joe Bartholomew, the first African American to design and build a public golf course in the United States, was not allowed to play on the courses he designed. The PGA banned Black golfers at its inception, not permitting an African American to compete in the U.S. Open until 1948. (Pinehurst would not admit Black members until 1970.) Although the resort supplied meals for the caddies for a fee, they ate in a separate dining room and did not mingle with white guests. African Americans were not allowed in the clubhouse.

When it comes to the depiction in local newspapers, the tendency is to romanticize the Pinehurst caddies as if they lived a rarified life, immune to segregation. Articles portray the relationship between African American caddies and their white bosses as mutually respectful and happy. An air of detached paternalism prevails: "They thought of themselves as part of our family, and we took care of them." Such was the attitude du jour. Nevertheless, caddies still had to bear the weight of bias. One *Greensboro News and Record* reporter notes that despite the airbrushed narratives of the Pinehurst caddie, the reality was that after they grew too old to walk the courses, many caddies, without Social Security benefits, "died in wretched poverty."

In Pinehurst, Black people were not allowed to work front-of-house in a hotel; all wait staff were white. African American women worked behind the scenes as maids or laundresses. Annie Oakley's husband, Frank Butler, once wrote to a friend that all the wait staff at the Carolina Hotel were white, a routine practice in all posh restaurants in the South. Black groundskeepers at Pinehurst's golf courses mainly worked during the off-season and before or after peak hours, so they would not interact with white guests. Pinehurst's Black workforce was largely unseen by design, except for its caddies.

Pinehurst caddie with lady golfer on sand green. *Wilson Special Collections Library, UNC–Chapel Hill.*

In addition to this enforced segregation, the demeaning myth of the "happy caddie" prevailed. Articles from the 1920s and 1930s are filled with the notion that African Americans were uniquely suited to carrying golf clubs and were delighted to do so. In a 1931 *Pinehurst Outlook* article, Bion Butler describes what he believes to be the unique traits of the Pinehurst caddie: "almost invariabl[y] good nature[d]….Even when he is stupid, he is funny." He knows how to accommodate the "white player's wants." Butler speaks of the caddie as an "attraction" and a "feature" of the Sandhills not to be missed, as if he is part of the local scenery. In a 1933 article, Butler writes, "It's funny how eternally happy they [caddies] are." He says Pinehurst caddies are better than northern caddies (usually white teenage boys) not because of their knowledge of the courses and game but because "they have no higher ambition other than to become good caddies." The village published the *Pinehurst Outlook*, so one can assume Butler's views reflected the village's.

Butler wasn't the only one to hold such paternalistic views. In a series of short articles published in 1931 and 1933, Frank Finney wrote about a character named "Doctor Buzzard." The stories recount the experiences of a fictional caddie from Southern Pines who subscribes to voodoo and other "root medicine." The article is replete with racial stereotypes: Finney describes "the coal-black darkie's good nature" and his supposed naïve superstitions. Photos of Black caddies accompany the report, suggesting that all caddies subscribe to voodoo practices. In one photo, an African American man, smartly dressed in a suit and fedora, has the words "Doctor Buzzard" below the image. Did such attitudes spill out onto the golf courses? It's hard to imagine they didn't.

Events like the cakewalk, beautiful baby contest, and Five Dollar Drive also fostered racist attitudes. Each year, the Pinehurst resort sponsored the "Caddie Rush" or "Five Dollar Drive." A golfer, usually a prominent resort member, would drive a ball as far as possible. (For instance, in 1914, President Joseph H. Appel of the Winter Golf League of Advertising Interests drove the ball for the caddie rush.) Then, caddies would race out after the ball. The person who retrieved the ball and returned it to the golfer first received five dollars. Such activities were no doubt demeaning, even if the instigators thought they were acting out of benevolence. It was in this environment that African American caddies made their living. One historian goes so far as to say that these activities "terrorized African Americans working at the resort."

Segregation did not end at the clubhouse. James Walker Tufts built the Lexington Hotel inside the village proper for his white employees, but African Americans lived a world apart in nearby Taylortown. In 1933, a local writer described Taylortown as "the world of dusky humanity that surrounds the village of Pinehurst" and assured readers that the lines between the two towns were "sharply drawn." In other words, there was a strict color line in the Sandhills. By and large, the golf world in the South perpetuated the racism of the times, and Pinehurst was no exception.

On the courses, rules were strict. Caddies quickly learned they must cooperate because "if they ever get a black mark on this course, they were blocked from ever caddying on any Pinehurst course." Is it any wonder the caddies appeared to be good-humored? An old photo album in the Tufts Archives, dated 1911, contains 170 black-and-white photographs of Pinehurst's African American caddies. Each man (or boy) sits in a chair and poses for his portrait. Penciled below some of the photographs, in elaborate cursive handwriting, are the words "good," "bad," "sorry" or discharged." No one knows where the book comes from or its purpose. Was this how the clubhouse management kept tabs on its caddies, culling out those who refused to play by the rules?

In the South, a white caddie master typically oversaw caddies to ensure they "acted, appeared, and performed their duties in a supportive but submissive way." Caddies also had to undergo yearly physical exams where they were vaccinated and checked for contagious diseases "to ensure they were fit for work with white golfers."

Much has been said of the relatively high wages a caddie could earn. But even though Pinehurst caddies could make about two to three dollars a day—much more than those who worked in the dairy or on the farm—they did not work every day or throughout the year. They still earned lower wages than their white counterparts. For instance, Pinehurst golfers paid their northern chauffeurs about thirty-five dollars weekly. "The low pay and seasonal work ensured a poverty-stricken life in the Sandhills," one historian concludes.

That's not to say, however, that there weren't acts of kindness extended to some caddies. A letter dated June 27, 1927, tells of a caddie arrested for possessing a firearm. Pinehurst Inc. recommended a fine rather than a prison sentence. In another letter, a boy whose father worked for the resort needed money to buy his family clothes. Pinehurst Inc. donated the articles the family needed. In 1940, when bad weather impeded golfing, affecting the caddies' income, members of the Tin Whistles organized to raise money for needy families.

Pinehurst caddie. *Wilson Special Collections Library, UNC–Chapel Hill.*

Pinehurst caddies playing golf. *Tufts Archives.*

In a time when Black people were ostensibly kept out of sight in Pinehurst, its caddies were front and center. Caddying allowed them advancement, and their skills became known and admired by golfers around the nation, especially on the notoriously tricky No. 2. Some local events celebrated the caddies, like the annual Caddie Tournament. At the season's close, one of the Pinehurst courses would be open for the Caddie Tournament. It was played yearly since 1935 (other records say 1939) and showcased the golf talent of the Pinehurst caddies, some of whom could have played professionally if not for racial barriers.

Another event was the Tom Cotton Annual Golf Tournament, named after Tom Cotton, who was a fixture at the Pinehurst Resort. Born into slavery in (or around) 1843, Cotton moved to Pinehurst in 1913 and did odd jobs for the resort, including groundskeeping. At one time, Cotton lived in the log cabin that is now the Sandhills Woman's Exchange. Around 1930, the Tom Cotton Club was formed in his honor; the group was made up primarily of employees of the Tufts organization. According to a former member, it was named after "Uncle Tom because he was a character around here. He was a symbol; he was well-liked."

In June 2001, Pinehurst caddies were recognized for their contributions to the resort with the establishment of a Caddie Hall of Fame. According to a program brochure for the induction ceremony, each caddie was selected for his "length of service, character and integrity, exceptional tournament

Tom Cotton, a Pinehurst favorite. *Wilson Special Collections Library, UNC–Chapel Hill.*

CADDIES DRESSED FOR THE NORTH AND SOUTH OPEN. THIS WAS FIRST YEAR THEY HAD ANYTHING LIKE A UNIFORM ___ ALL HAD MATCHING SWEATERS. MAN BEHIND GOLF BAG IS BUDDY LOVE.

Pinehurst caddies at the North and South. *Tufts Archives.*

"The Caddie," by Edgar A. Guest
Pinehurst Outlook, April 27, 1922, page 12

It was a little caddie boy who said to me
    in shame:
"I've beaten many a man at golf, and
    never won a game."
"You've beaten many a man," said I,
    "and yet you say to me
You've never won a single game? That surely cannot be."

"I beat my man today," said he,
    "At least he swore I did;
He dubbed three shots on Number Seven,
    and said: 'Confound you, kid!
I wish you wouldn't stand so near when
    I am set to play; a
I've told you half a dozen times to
    Keep out of my way.'

"Three years I've caddied at the club
    and twice a week or more
I've had to tote the losers' bags and
    always they were sore
And always they have made it plain upon
    the eighteenth tee
That they'd have won the game hands
    down if it hadn't been for me.

"It seems I always beat the man who
    plays a rotten game,
And every time he dubs a shot I have to
    take the blame;
But when that fellow wins a match he's
    proud as he can be
And takes the credit all himself and never
    mentions me."

Pinehurst caddies with golfers. *Wilson Special Collections Library, UNC–Chapel Hill.*

performance." Each had to be "an upstanding citizen of the community and a long-term contributor to Pinehurst's caddie program." The inaugural class of inductees included Fletcher Gaines, Robert "Hardrock" Robinson, Jimmy Steed, Teddy Marley, Robert Stafford, Hilton "Doctor" Rogers, John T. Daniel "Barney Google," Jack Williams, Jeff "Ratman" Ferguson, and Willie McRae. Caddies have been part of Pinehurst's storied past, and the hall of fame was designed to honor those who made playing golf in Pinehurst such a unique experience. Over the years, more and more names have been added to the roster.

The following are profiles of some of Pinehurst's earliest and most famous caddies.

Jimmy Steed

Jimmy Steed was a Pinehurst caddie since 1912. He was Sam Snead's favorite caddie, so Steed traveled with him when he started playing the professional circuit. Snead knew Steed was essential when playing on No. 2: "You have to have two heads on the course," he once remarked. In 1971, Snead won the PGA Club Pro Championship in Pinehurst. Steed is credited with helping Snead win three North and South Championships. "Sam had a great many talents, but one of them was NOT selecting clubs," says Bill Campbell, a noted competitor of the era. "Jimmy had the knack of giving Sam the right clubs."

Robert "Hardrock" Robinson

Born in 1914, Robert Robinson, or "Hardrock" as his friends called him, started caddying in Pinehurst in the 1920s. Robinson caddied for many golf greats like Ben Hogan and Walter Hagen and was known for keeping players calm. According to one source, Robinson "had an engaging personality which, added to his quick study of the game and Pinehurst's tricky greens, came to the notice of Ross, who asked Robinson to become his caddy." He had a close relationship with Donald Ross and became his personal caddie and then an assistant, running errands and doing other jobs for him. Robinson said that Donald Ross "wouldn't play golf unless I caddied for him" and intimated that other caddies resented his close relationship with the boss. Robinson spent a lot of time with Ross and knew that the Scot did not like it when someone scored well on his beloved No. 2. The next day, the two would be on the links looking for ways to tweak the course to make it more difficult.

Robinson was a good golfer and once shot a 64 on Pinehurst No. 1 and won the Caddie Tournament one year. After hours, Robinson would walk the courses looking for lost balls, which he would wash and resell to players. He was the only caddie allowed to do this.

No one knows how he got his nickname, but two stories surface. The first is that Robinson was called "Hardrock" because he liked to tap dance on top of a barrel but never injured himself if he fell off. His head, they said, was as hard as a rock. The second story is that his father called him "Hardrock" because Robert liked rock candy. Robinson had an eight-piece band called the Midnight Hawks. In 1938, his band was such a hit at the gymkhana

Pinehurst caddies band. *Tufts Archives.*

held at the Carolina Inn that they were booked for the rest of the season. Robinson's washtub band also greeted guests at the Southern Pines train station. Robinson was proud that he was also in a 1927 movie, *The Sun Sets in Pinehurst*, starring Gloria Swanson.

FLETCHER GAINES

It's not unusual for caddies to also be excellent golfers, and this was true of Fletcher Gaines, who caddied at Pinehurst since 1938. Many believe Gaines could have played the PGA tour if they had admitted African Americans, but he did play on the Black golf tour throughout the East Coast. He won seven consecutive Pinehurst Caddie Tournaments and ten overall. Gaines could earn more money playing in Charleston and Columbia, where prize purses were $600 to $700. (The Pinehurst prize was a mere $15.) Gaines regularly played Pinehurst No. 2 below par.

In his first few years at Pinehurst, Gaines recalls that the resort used to get them out of school when the season got busy and that they sometimes got paid in "slips," which could be used at the department store. This was during the Great Depression, and the scrip money helped people put food on the table, he recalled.

Pinehurst caddies with golfers. *Wilson Special Collections Library, UNC–Chapel Hill.*

In his day, Gaines was the most requested caddie at Pinehurst. He was on the bag for the 1936 PGA Championship held in Pinehurst, the 1951 Ryder Cup and for ten winners of the North and South. His knowledge of No. 2 was second to none. "I would tell them, you're playing the course, but I know it," Gaines added.

Like many Pinehurst caddies, Gaines carried clubs for many golf greats, including Julius Boros, Tommy Armour, and Curtis Strange. In back-to-back years (1975–76), Strange won the North and South, with Gaines as his caddie. Later, Strange remarked, "It was you and I as a team that brought out the best in each of us. You are a wonderful caddie but a better person." Past director of golf Don Padgett called Gaines "a national gem." He added, "When you opt to have him by your side, you've got one of the great friends of Pinehurst walking down the fairway with you."

John T. Daniel "Barney Google"

John Daniel, or "Barney Google," is best known for helping Harvie Ward win the 1948 North and South Championship. "Ward didn't beat Stranahan today," one spectator recalled, "Barney Google did." As one reporter said, "His golf-gripped mind seems to have a mental picture of every blade of grass, and few who followed the match will deny that it was Harvey's hands and eyes coupled with Barney's judgment that was making the putts drop as they did."

Wille McRae

Pinehurst's most famous caddie, Willie McRae, said that his father taught him that the way to succeed as a Pinehurst caddie was to "show up, keep up, and shut up." Four generations of McRaes have caddied at Pinehurst. Willie started in 1943 when he was just ten years old, learning first from his father and then from "Hardrock" Robinson. Willie would go on to caddie at Pinehurst for seventy-five years and reportedly knew No. 2 better than anyone. "He could read the green before the ball stopped rolling on your approach shot," one golfer observed. So renowned was he that according to resort management, when anyone famous came to Pinehurst to play golf, they wanted Willie on the bag. McRae caddied for Donald Ross, Yogi Berra, Michael Jordan, Peyton Manning, Bobby Jones, Gene Sarazen, Arnold Palmer, and four U.S. presidents. (He says Gerald Ford was the best golfer of the four.) He was the caddie for Fred Daley during the 1951 Ryder Cup.

McRae will tell you that the key to his success was keeping players happy, which, he said, is very hard to do on the notoriously tricky No. 2. One golfer remarked, "He's great at reading greens. He was a little bit of a teacher and he has a good sense of humor and is easy to talk to." Ben Crenshaw noted, "Willie was always highly sought after by so many fine players who played Pinehurst and returned there. He knew the golf course [No. 2] better than anyone." Ross's courses often had optical illusions, so the caddie had to read the greens, the spine of the roll and how the grass leans to the sun. And no one did that better than Willie McRae.

This expertise did not come by observation alone, though. McRae spent hours studying the courses: "I used to walk all the Pinehurst greens on my own time so that I'd know how the ball would break from any point."

Above: Pinehurst golfers, caddies, and gallery. *Wilson Special Collections Library, UNC–Chapel Hill.*

Left: Plaque of Hall of Fame caddies, Pinehurst Country Club. *Photo by author.*

McRae understood the value of having close contact with the land: "Golf is supposed to be a walking sport, not a riding sport. If you're walking to the ball, you got time to think. When you're riding down there so fast, you ain't got time to think. That's why you hit so many bad shots."

He knew how to keep his players loose and relaxed, having a stock of jokes ready. Even though he was barred from playing at Pinehurst Country Club because of his race, he was the only caddie permitted to use a cart on No. 2 when he got on in years.

Despite his status at the resort, McRae was not immune to racial prejudice. He recalls a player becoming irate after a lousy shot and throwing his club, which ended up in a tree. He insisted that McRae get it down, but Willie responded, "I'm not getting paid to climb trees. If you want it, you better go get it." He noticed that some players "thought they owned you and the golf course…younger people and middle-aged people are a whole lot better than they were back in the 40s." As for the Tufts family, McRae has only praise, saying that James and Leonard Tufts "never forgot the contribution African Americans had made here. The Tufts all treated us well."

McRae's memories are recorded in his book, *On the Bag: Seventy Years Remembered by Pinehurst's Hall-of-Fame Caddie.* Wille recalls caddying for Bobby Jones when he was fourteen. Naturally, the young caddie hesitated to advise the famous player, but Jones encouraged him to be assertive. "He always talked to me like I was somebody," McRae added. In fact, McRae became friends with many of the great golfers of his day: "I didn't just carry their golf bags, I got to talk to them…really know them as men." He remembers Walter Hagen kicking back shots of Johnnie Walker Red during one round of golf and said that Hagen was fun to be around because he kept things lighthearted. He remembered giving pointers to President Harry Truman and being paired with Sugar Ray Leonard once for a round of golf.

After nearly eight decades working alongside an array of golfers, from novices to professionals, Rae concludes, "Great people exist at every level, and every level has its share of jerks.…To me, everybody's a celebrity. Everybody is special in their unique way."

Chapter 3

THE SANDHILLS WOMAN'S EXCHANGE

Helping others to help themselves.
—motto of the National Federation of Woman's Exchanges

When Boston native Katharine Tuckerman attended the annual Sandhills Fair in Pinehurst in 1922, she was bowled over. On display at the Ladies Auxiliary Home Demonstration were beautiful, handcrafted goods made by local farm women: intricate rugs, baskets and quilts; colorful dolls and toys; and sumptuous jams, jellies, and preserves. Tuckerman, who had learned about the National Federation of Woman's Exchanges in Boston, wondered if she might start a group in the Sandhills.

The National Federation of Woman's Exchanges is a benevolent society that started in Philadelphia in 1832 and quickly spread throughout the United States. The basic idea was simple: women consigned their handiwork to a central location (the Exchange) to earn extra income. At a time when job opportunities were limited, especially for those in rural areas, the Exchange provided a way for women to support their families. Tuckerman had the idea, and the rural women had the handicrafts. Next, they needed a group of energetic women to kick off the organization. Not one to drag her feet, Tuckerman assembled the first official meeting at Mrs. E.W. Merrill's house in Pinehurst on May 2, 1923.

The ten founding members initially met at various members' homes, selling the consigned goods on the porch of the Way House on Pee Dee Road

Original cabin of Sandhills Woman's Exchange. *Moore County Historical Association.*

Darthea Cowgill. *Used by permission of Meriwether Cowgill Schmid.*

in Knollwood. But as the Exchange grew, Tuckerman realized they needed a permanent place, hopefully in a central location. Gertrude Tufts, who served as the first vice chairman of the Sandhills Woman's Exchange (SWE), suggested using the deserted log cabin on Azalea Road. Notes from the December 12, 1923 meeting indicate that there was an "informal discussion about the exchange being kept in the log cabin in Pinehurst. Mrs. Tufts was to investigate and report later." Next month, the cabin was again brought up. Gertrude reported that her husband, Leonard, might be willing to repair the cabin and rent it to the Exchange at a reduced rate. It's unknown what transpired in the ensuing months—perhaps some arm-twisting on Gertrude's part—but within the year, Leonard Tufts had donated the cabin to the SWE. They held their first meeting in the tiny log cabin on November 12, 1924.

Although Gertrude Tufts was instrumental in securing the cabin for the Exchange, she remained vice chairman only for a few months. It was the combined effort of three women, Molly Lovering, Darthea Cowgill, and Katharine Tuckerman, that got the Exchange off the ground. Lovering excelled at teaching new crafts, Cowgill had a car and could run delivery to and from the Exchange, and Tuckerman organized the whole enterprise. The three were the organization's backbone, serving together for over twenty years.

THE LOG CABIN

The log cabin itself has a fascinating history. Seemingly out of place in a village known for its elegant Federal-style architecture, the original log structure, built in 1823 by James Ray, ended up in Pinehurst simply because James Walker Tufts fancied it. While records vary—either Tufts purchased the cabin from the Archibald McKenzie family, or they donated it to him—he nonetheless relocated the ramshackle building to the pine grove on Azalea Road. The McKenzies had used the building as a kitchen, and so Tufts built them a new kitchen as a parting gesture.

Once Tufts had the cabin spruced up, he used it as a town museum, displaying local artifacts. But after James Walker's death, son Leonard rented out the property to a formerly enslaved person named Jerry Mitchell, who was caretaker of the pine grove, the deer park, and the village grounds. At that time, the village was encircled by a six-foot fence used to keep out wild boar and other animals, and it was one of Mitchell's jobs to ensure that the fence gates were always closed. When Mitchell vacated,

Uncle Mitchell's Cabin in the Pine Park.   Pinehurst, N. C.

Jerry Mitchell outside cabin. *Wikimedia Commons.*

Tom Cotton and his brother Charlie, also formerly enslaved, moved into the cabin. The brothers moved out in 1923, and the building was left vacant, eventually falling into disrepair. After Tufts made some necessary repairs, the Sandhills Woman's Exchange moved into the building and has occupied the site ever since. That same year, Mrs. Crocker (Darthea's mother) donated $500, a princely sum, to build a sorely needed addition to the one-room cabin.

The Exchange stands as a testament to the women's philanthropy and volunteerism. Not only did they meet bimonthly to discuss matters like fundraising, advertising and business practices, but some, like Lovering and Cowgill, spent many hours driving out to the rural homesteads—no easy feat on the sandy, pitted roads—to obtain the consigners' work and bring them back to the Exchange. When necessary, the pair also went to the women's homes to teach them new crafts or new recipes. Members donated extra material to the consignors. Early on, some even fronted the crafters money so they could build up inventory. Remembering that these efforts were voluntary, one marvels at the dedication of the SWE members. During their first year in the cabin, the SWE netted a profit of about $1,300, a considerable sum in the 1920s.

Darthea Cowgill's daughter, Meriwether Schmid, ninety-six, now living in Florida, still remembers her trips to Pinehurst and her mother's involvement

Cabin with new addition. *Moore County Historical Association.*

with the Exchange. When asked if she thought the consignors included Black women, Schmid says she doesn't know. But because the South was segregated during the Jim Crow era, she thinks it's unlikely that the Exchange accepted consignments from the African American community. Indeed, there is no evidence to indicate that Black women were included in the consignors' circle.

The Tufts Archives house the SWE's original handwritten minutes from 1924 until the 1970s. Reading through the minutes, one cannot help but notice the business acumen of the committee members. They had intense discussions about how to maximize profits. They talked about adjusting prices and improving displays. They experimented with hours of operation, markup costs, transportation of goods, and ways to cut expenses to benefit the consigners. For instance, they discovered that "Wednesdays should be cake and candy day at the Exchange." Food remained a best seller (as it does today). The minutes tell the story of a well-run business that grew and flourished, even through the Great Depression and World War II.

At the onset, the SWE had about forty consignors. Three years later, they were up to fifty-nine. In less than five years, the Exchange had to hire two paid workers, an administrator and a cook, to accommodate their growth. Personal donations trickled in. In 1924, the members voted to install a telephone on the premises. Telephones were uncommon in rural North

Original cabin with villagers. *Moore County Historical Association.*

Carolina then, so adding this new technology speaks to the Exchange's forward-thinking policies.

Peppered throughout the minutes are traces of humor. There's talk of the mice "eating up their profits" and of a roof that doesn't leak, or "hardly ever." The secretary notes that someone finally offered to dispose of our "white elephant"—a particularly ugly quilt that had been on sale at the Exchange for two years. Absent is the lofty sense of noblesse oblige one often finds in Progressive-era do-gooders. These prominent Pinehurst women wanted to help those in need and weren't afraid to roll up their sleeves. An excerpt from a letter written by Darthea Cowgill in 1923 reveals their concern:

> *I imagine living 17 miles from the tiniest town, caring for 2 cows, 4–8 children and all the yearly budget depending on whether the tobacco and cotton crops were good or poor and suddenly finding by spending a few hours a week hooking rugs out of thread bare garments or knitting cotton gloves for the more fortunate who hunted to hounds, that you could have from $5 to $200 a month to spend.*

Loom and weaver. *Wilson Special Collections Library, UNC–Chapel Hill.*

Most rural families did not have running water, indoor plumbing or electricity. So Cowgill understood that money earned from consignments could go a long way to improving the lives of rural folks.

Like all business ventures, the Exchange constantly worked to improve its advertising. At one of their first meetings, the women decided to place large signs in strategic places throughout the village, like billboards, to draw people in. At the same time, they also distributed small cards to individuals. Plans were in the works to host a fundraiser at the Carolina Hotel. And as always, there was a push to drive up membership.

Open for Business

Another way that the Exchange sought to bring in customers was by using a mannequin dressed up as a "colored Mammy." Since 1927, the papier-mâché mannequin was set out on the front porch (or by the front gate) to signal that the Exchange was open for business. Historically, in the southern United States, the mammy was a stereotype of an African American nursemaid or domestic. "Mammy" was often depicted as a heavy-set Black woman with a broad smiling face and a handkerchief on her head. To get the image in mind, one need only think of Aunt Jemima on a syrup bottle or Hattie McDaniel's character, Mammy, in the film *Gone with the Wind.*

We learn about the "Mammy's" origin from meeting minutes dated February 9, 1927. Member Grace Whittemore proposed "dressing a tall figure as a colored Mammy" and placing it at the gate to encourage passersby to stop in. The members must have seconded the motion because the secretary commends Mrs. Whittemore at the next meeting for the "colored mammy which she made." They used the prop immediately, noting that it caused "a great deal of interest." If they wanted people to stop and enter the cabin, then "Mammy" was doing the trick. (According to longtime residents of Pinehurst, "Mammy" also served as a de facto weather report. If it were on the porch, it would rain. If by the front gate, you could expect a sunny day.)

It's curious why a progressive organization like the Sandhills Woman's Exchange would use such a tactic. How would this draw people in? And why use this particular figure?

First, it was familiar. According to cultural historian David Pilgrim, the mammy image was used extensively in advertising in American material culture, especially for baking and cooking products. Pilgrim writes:

> *Mammy was born on the plantation in the imagination of slavery defenders, but she grew in popularity during the period of Jim Crow. The mainstreaming of Mammy was primarily, but not exclusively, the result of the fledgling advertising industry. The mammy image was used to sell almost any household item, especially breakfast foods, detergents, planters, ashtrays, sewing accessories, and beverages. As early as 1875, Aunt Sally, a Mammy image, appeared on baking powder cans. Later, different Mammy images appeared on Luzianne coffee and cleaners, Fun to Wash detergent, Aunt Dinah molasses, and other products. Mammy represented wholesomeness. You can trust the mammy pitchwoman.*

So perhaps the women chose this familiar figure because it was associated with domesticity and cooking. But there may be another reason.

As appalling as it may sound today, in 1927, the mammy figure was "trending." The year Mrs. Whittemore created "Mammy" for the Exchange, Al Jolson starred in the film *The Jazz Singer.* Jolson, in blackface, sang the sentimental song "My Mammy," which became wildly popular with audiences. Perhaps the women of the SWE wanted to capitalize on the song's popularity.

While familiarity and trends may have had something to do with it, the real reason the Exchange used "Mammy" is revealed in minutes filed deep within the archives. It's a fascinating part of Pinehurst's hidden history.

In 1948, Tuckerman, Lovering and Cowgill attended a SWE meeting on April 9. During that meeting, as they reminisced about the early days of the Exchange, Katharine Tuckerman revealed something astonishing about "Mammy":

> *Mrs. Tuckerman emphasized the fact that visitors from the north like to feel they are in the South, and the more southern atmosphere the better they like it. They all enjoy buying things with a distinct southern flavor and in a southern atmosphere and the cabin was planned with that in mind. The entrance, with its big fireplace and fire tools and other "old South" equipment keynoted the Exchange, with the help of Mammy, who was acquired in 1927.*

In other words, "Mammy" was part of a tableau designed to attract *northerners* and to appeal to their sense of the "old South." Recall that most of the visitors to the village, especially in its early days, were from the North. Grace Whittemore herself was from Brookline, Massachusetts. Perhaps in her mind, this caricature of the Old South would appeal to fellow northerners, urging them to stop at the Exchange and support its work. Without the meeting minutes, we would never understand why the members of the Exchange chose this particular image to display on its porch. Using such a racial caricature for advertisement speaks to the racial dynamics of time and place.

We do not know when the SWE stopped using the mannequin. A note from November 1941 indicates that the figure received an updated wardrobe:

> *Then "Mammy" all resplendent in her new red dress and bonnet with new white apron,—seemed just too attractive to leave alone and unprotected,— in the midst of all these war maneuvers. Not wishing her captured by "Reds or Blues"—Miss Ward travelled to Aberdeen—procured a strong padlock and chain. And now "Mammy" is safely attached to the picket fence.*

So it's evident that "Mammy" was used at least until World War II. Some suggest that "Mammy" was put into storage in the library basement when the Tufts Archives were created in 1965, but a photo from *The Pilot*, a Southern Pines newspaper, indicates otherwise.

An article about the SWE from 1977 is accompanied by a photo of two executive members standing next to "Mammy." The caption reads, "One of the colored ladies that stands on the porch of the Sandhills Woman's Exchange." Meeting minutes from March of the same year indicate that the women had talked about discontinuing the use of the display but decided to keep using the figure "as it has for many years." So it's clear that the figure was in use at least until 1977.

Four years later, the SWE "Mammy" was stolen. At that juncture, members talked about replacing the figure with a "mountain girl," but they made no decision. Minutes from October 20, 1981, indicate that the members decided to take up a collection for "Mammy's" return reward. They raised ninety-one dollars. At that meeting, the idea of replacing the stolen figure with a "mountain-type figure" was again floated. They were still discussing these options four months later. By April 18, 1982, the members of the SWE had decided on the mountain lady. But they did not carry out their plans because there is no material evidence of such a mannequin—no photos, written records, or newspaper articles. So, according to the archival records, the last time "Mammy" was in use was October 1981. Curiously, meeting minutes dated October 14, 1983, indicate that members were still discussing a name for "the new mammy." It's unclear if the old one had been found or if they had decided to install a new mannequin. The SWE "Mammy" does not come up again in the meeting minutes, and no one seems to know what happened to the original mannequin.

Whatever the case, the figure had been associated with the Exchange for more than fifty years. What had begun as a way to appeal to a northerner's concept of the Old South during the Jim Crow era was part and parcel of the Exchange's identity until 1981. The mannequin—whether the original one or a replacement—is currently in storage at the Tufts Archives.

Keeping Pace with the Times

Unlike many American businesses, the Sandhills Woman's Exchange stayed afloat during the Great Depression. Indeed, consignors relied more than ever on the income generated from the sales. One reason for their continued success was the quality of the consigned goods. The Receiving and Pricing Committee saw to that. Handwoven products were best

Rug makers. *Wilson Special Collections Library, UNC–Chapel Hill.*

sellers, along with hooked rugs. The Exchange sold forty-five hooked or handwoven rugs in one month. These rugs were so exquisite that they garnered praise from a purchaser in New York City. Meeting minutes reveal, "The head rug buyer from Altman's in New York called at the Exchange and remarked about our hooked rugs, saying they were the best she had seen in the South." Sandhills rugs were now being sold in the most luxurious department store in New York City.

Month after month, committees met to discuss how to boost profits for the consignors and save money on operations. Volunteers lavishly decorated the cabin for Christmas, recognizing that sales skyrocketed during the holidays. They honed their advertising strategies, relying on events like a fashion show to raise money. And they kept a close eye on accounts. In 1930, despite shortages in food and material and a downtick in consignment sales, food sales tripled. A year later, they hired a bookkeeper to keep pace with the accounting. As always, they knew which items sold and which did not. Hot ticket items in 1933 included "knitted sports suit and skirts," with Mrs. Donald Ross overseeing the Knitting Committee.

Even though sales and personnel had grown, the SWE members were mindful not to lose touch with consignors. In addition to the annual

Potter. *Wilson Special Collections Library, UNC–Chapel Hill.*

meeting with the executive board and consignors, the members also started a new committee "to renew the old closeness and to exchange ideas and suggestions for the work." Communication was key. Because few farms had telephones, volunteers at the Exchange conveyed important information to the farm women via postcards.

Handmade pottery. *Wilson Special Collections Library, UNC–Chapel Hill.*

Despite the Exchange's best efforts, the 1930s were lean years for rural women. Out of 239 consignors, 56 made no sales at all. Recognizing how the Depression ravaged poor farmers, the Exchange decided that consignors with no sales were exempt from paying the next year's annual registration fee. When ninety dollars' worth of goods were stolen, the executive committee decided to pay the consignors for the stolen goods without letting anyone know. An elderly Sandhills resident who grew up in the 1930s said that his mother would not have been able to feed her eleven children without the money she earned at the Exchange.

During World War II, despite food shortages and reduced hours, the SWE flourished. Materials were in short supply: there was never enough butter or sugar, thanks to rations, and they had to economize gasoline consumption. But out-of-state sales were increasing, and the consignors now came from outside the Sandhills. By 1941, less than half of the artisans were from Moore County. All in all, the SWE did what it could during wartime. They cut back on hours, curtailed monthly meetings, and reduced dues for families with service members in the war.

Despite the hard times, sales remained brisk. A financial report recording sales from 1940 to 1944 showed an "almost phenomenal increase in business in this time." As a result, the consignors were receiving larger checks than ever. One can only imagine what this extra income meant for rural families during the war.

Volunteers from the American Red Cross came to the Exchange to solicit donations for the soldiers at Fort Bragg (now Fort Liberty). Books, games, cards, blankets, sweaters, socks, and "knit[ted] knee rugs for wheelchairs" were especially desired. According to meeting minutes dated February 13, 1942, the need at Fort Bragg hospitals was "very great at present and ever increasing." What consignors could not sell, they often donated to the hospitals on base.

By the time the 1950s rolled around, the Exchange was well established. There were rumblings about adding a tearoom, but the superior beverage won out. On January 15, 1957, the Coffee Room was opened. This new addition came with more responsibilities: complying with county health regulations and planning a fresh daily menu. Notes from this period take on a business rather than philanthropic tone; numbers and figures dominate the narrative rather than personal stories. But the Exchange was run with the same energy and efficiency as ever.

National Register of Historic Places

In 1996, the cabin was placed in the National Register of Historic Places along with other historic buildings in Pinehurst Village. But in 2015, the board voted to close the Exchange permanently for insufficient funds. "We had $16 left in the checking account," then manager of the Exchange Carole Southon recalls. Pinehurst would lose an important part of its history. But thanks to tireless efforts, spearheaded by Cav Peterson and helped along by numerous members of the community, the Exchange went through a revitalization process. It held a flurry of fundraisers—fashion shows, bridal fashion shows, and teas aboard a historic train car. The local football team showed up to clean the cabin and prepare it for its annual fall opening. Within two years, the Exchange was back on its feet, enjoying a measure of financial security.

In 2022, the Exchange celebrated its centennial. The organization has done so well that members not only support local artisans, but they also give back to the community via donations to nonprofit organizations. According to the latest data from the Federation of Woman's Exchanges, the Sandhills chapter is one of only fifteen Exchanges left in the United States. While you might not see a hooked rug for sale in the cabin, you will find handcrafted jewelry, pottery, pine needle baskets, knitted and crocheted items, and other goods. The Exchange still has a busy "cabin café" with homecooked meals at a decent price—plan to wait for a table during peak hours. (The wait staff are all volunteers; even their tips go to the Exchange.) The SWE also sponsors educational programs called "lunch and learns" on everything from starting a container garden to making chocolate mousse. The small fee benefits the Exchange.

The Exchange today. *Photo Kristin Stevens.*

The SWE soldiers on, with two full-time staff members—a cook and a manager—and an army of volunteers. Their motto, "helping others help themselves," remains at the core as it did a century ago when the Exchange first moved into the tiny log cabin on Azalea Road.

Chapter 4

ANNIE OAKLEY

God intended women to be outside as well as men, and they do not know what
they are missing when they stay cooped up in the house with a novel.
—Annie Oakley

She was considered the best woman shooter of her day and the first female superstar. At the height of her fame, she earned more money per year than the president of the United States. Touring with Buffalo Bill's Wild West Show, Annie Oakley enjoyed international fame. But in her retirement, Oakley wanted to retreat from the crowds and enjoy some hunting with her husband, Frank Butler. Partial to refined society, Oakley found Pinehurst, North Carolina, to her liking. She and Frank wintered there for seven seasons (1915–22), living at the Carolina Hotel and Thistle Cottage. She gave free shooting lessons to women while he oversaw the skeet and trap range. Friends of Leonard and Gertrude Tufts, the Butlers were part of the village social scene from the onset, attending parties and dances. They loved the mild weather and the abundance of shooting, hunting, and riding. Most weeks, Oakley joined the weekly fox hunt, rising at four o'clock in the morning to meet the other riders. Now in her fifties, Oakley said these hunts kept her "vital." But life had not always been fox hunts and high society for Annie.

Born on August 13, 1860, in Darke County, Ohio, Oakley, whose legal name was Phoebe Ann Moses (or Mozee or Mosey), was one of eight children raised by devout Quaker parents. Annie embodied traditional

Left: Young Annie Oakley. *Wikimedia Commons.*

Below: Annie Oakley at Pinehurst Gun Club. *Wilson Special Collections Library, UNC–Chapel Hill.*

Quaker values her whole life, putting her family first, working hard, and valuing humility and honesty. Annie's father died when she was five, leaving her family destitute. Unable to support all her children, Annie's mother, Susanah, sent her to the Darke County Infirmary in Greenville, Ohio, where Annie learned how to sew, embroider, read, and write. Oakley never forgot those years, and when she became famous, she often gave out free tickets to children, especially orphans.

When she was twelve, Annie was sent to live with a well-to-do farm couple. Oakley's experience with them reads like something out of a Dickens novel. The couple promised that Annie would only have to look after their three-year-old son and that she would have time to attend school and trap and shoot. Instead, they worked her nearly to death. Once, when Annie had fallen asleep while darning socks, the wife woke her up violently. She tossed Annie into the cold, snowy night, where she almost froze. Oakley never revealed their names but called them "the wolves."

She endured the cruelty of the wolves for two years but finally ran away, returning to her mother. Susanah discovered the scars on Annie's shoulder and back from the beatings. Though her mother had remarried, the family still struggled and could not afford to support Annie. So, Annie was sent back to the infirmary in Greenville, where she stayed until she was fifteen. By then, Annie was contributing to the family income by shooting game birds and selling them at the local market. Her days at the infirmary and with the wolves were soon over.

From an early age, Annie loved the outdoors. No one knows when she first picked up a gun, but by the time she was fifteen, Annie had garnered a reputation as a sure shot. Store owners in Greenville who bought her game were getting requests for Annie's animals because the meat had no buckshot in it. (She downed her prey with one shot to the head.) Annie earned enough money from her shooting to pay off the mortgage on her mother's house. Around this time, she met Frank Butler, a man who would change her life.

Frank Butler

In the nineteenth century, sharpshooting was essential for frontier survival, but it was also a form of popular entertainment, especially on the vaudeville circuit. While accounts vary, sometime in the spring of 1880, a well-known sharpshooter named Frank Butler was putting on an exhibition near Greenville when locals suggested that he compete against their own sharpshooter. The prize was $100. Frank assented. He got the shock of his life when a girl just five feet tall stepped forward. "I almost dropped dead when a little slim girl in short dresses stepped out to the mark with me," he said. Annie won the contest, shooting twenty-five out of twenty-five live targets to Butler's twenty-four. She won the $100 prize and Butler's heart. They married the following year.

Shortly after their marriage, she changed her name to "Annie Oakley" and performed as Butler's assistant in his variety act because sharpshooting was strictly the purview of men. But when his partner fell ill one evening,

Frank asked Annie to step in. Her shooting skills captivated the audience. Butler knew a sure thing when he saw it, and soon after, he made Annie his stage partner. The couple toured with the Sells Brothers Circus as Butler and Oakley.

Over time, Butler recognized that Annie was the real star, so he stepped aside and made her the headliner. Butler became Annie's manager, teaching her stagecraft, especially how to play to an audience. One trick he taught her was to miss a target on purpose and then to pout mightily. The sympathetic audience would cheer wildly to spur on the young girl. Oakley would then manage to hit every target. The audience loved it. In reality, Oakley was so accurate with a gun she could shoot dimes out of the air and a lit cigarette out of Frank's mouth. In 1884, she hit 943 out of 1,000 glass balls in the air using a .22-caliber rifle. Oakley could shoot with both hands.

In 1884, the great Sioux chief Sitting Bull saw Oakley perform. He was so impressed that he adopted her as his daughter, a Native American custom given to those who are believed to possess unusual gifts. Oakley recalled that after her performance, "He concluded this was good medicine and that nothing short of a benevolent genius could make a fellow so accurate with a rifle." He nicknamed her "Watanya Cecilia" or "Little Sure Shot." The nickname stuck. Oakley recalled that Sitting Bull had given her "the full head-dress and the beaded moccasins the old warrior wore at Custer's land stand…and the worn and polished bow and quiver of arrows he clung to and used for killing game long after the advent of the rifle of in his tribe." When Sitting Bull gave Annie eighty dollars, all the money he had, she returned the gift.

In 1885, Annie Oakley signed on with Buffalo Bill's Wild West Show, quickly becoming its star attraction. It's difficult to fathom how popular the Wild West Show was, but one estimate gives an audience total of about

Annie Oakley in Europe. *Wikimedia Commons.*

one million spectators—per year! While traveling with the show, Oakley was billed as the "best shot that ever came out of the west." Never mind that she was from Ohio.

In 1887, the Wild West Show toured Europe, and it was there that Oakley became an international star. She was the toast of the town in London and Paris. Gifts, cards, flowers, and the occasional marriage proposal poured in. Oakley could sometimes be sharp-tongued. When a French count sent Annie a photograph and a marriage proposal in the mail, she promptly returned it. But first, she shot the picture in the head "where the brains should have been" and wrote "respectfully declined" across the chest. When performing, Oakley always used her stage name, and many fans didn't even know she was married. (It's believed that she chose the name "Oakley" because it was the name of the town where she first met Butler, although no one knows for sure.)

THE BUTLERS WERE MORE than ten years into their retirement—Annie was fifty-five, Frank sixty-five—when they chose to winter in Pinehurst. They had considered other resort towns in Florida but settled on Pinehurst because they thought it more "genteel" than other places, and the Sandhills offered abundant opportunities to hunt and ride. The couple arrived in November

Some of Oakley's Shooting Skills
- Shoot flames off a candle as they rotated on a wheel at fifty feet
- Shoot a lit cigarette from Frank's lips
- Shoot an apple off a dog's head
- Shoot glass balls, coins, and marbles tossed in the air
- Hit the thin edge of a card at ninety paces
- Put six shots in a playing card before it hits the ground
- Shoot over her shoulder, looking into a mirror, and with both hands
- Shoot the ace of hearts in the center heart

Annie Oakley shooting a target over her shoulder. *Wikimedia Commons.*

Top, left: Annie Oakley hunting quail. *Wikimedia Commons.*

Top, right: Annie Oakley giving shooting lessons to a woman. *Wikimedia Commons.*

Bottom: Annie Oakley at Pinehurst Gun Club. *Moore County Historical Association.*

and left in April, staying at the Carolina Inn and Thistle Cottage. (Reportedly, their beloved dog, Dave, was the only canine to be registered for a room at the posh Carolina Hotel.) Each morning, you could find Oakley sitting in a rocking chair on the front porch of the Carolina, reading her Bible and doing embroidery. It's hardly the picture of a world-famous gunslinger.

During her years in Pinehurst, Oakley taught an estimated 2,500 ladies how to use firearms at the hotel shooting range and the Pinehurst Gun

Club. The *Pinehurst Outlook* printed announcements that Oakley would give free shooting lessons every day from 11:00 a.m. to 12:00 noon. Prizes for the best scores were given out on Saturdays. Oakley firmly believed women should know how to use firearms to protect themselves. She never charged for the lessons but only hoped that women would become "shooting enthusiasts." She once quipped, "Powdering the face is not the same class as facing the powder."

Although in her fifties, she was still in peak condition during her Pinehurst years. Not only did she participate in weekly fox hunts, but she also raced at the jockey club and performed in amateur theatricals. She once remarked, "Any woman who does not thoroughly enjoy tramping across the country on a clear frosty morning with a good gun and a pair of dogs, does not know how to enjoy life." But Oakley was also partial to polite society and was not above mingling with the rich and famous, men like John Philip Sousa, Theodore Roosevelt, Booth Tarkington, and Will Rogers.

From 1915 to 1922, the Butlers managed the Pinehurst Gun Club. Some believe that Oakley did her best shooting there. In 1922, her last year in North Carolina, Annie shot one hundred out of one hundred clay targets at the sixteen-yard mark, setting a new world record for female shooters. She was sixty-two.

MEMORIES OF ANNIE OAKLEY

Looking through old issues of the *Outlook*, one can't help but notice that Oakley was Pinehurst's A-list celebrity. Everything she did made headlines. Aside from the usual coverage of her shooting exhibitions, the *Outlook* also published a series of unique articles called "Memories of Annie Oakley," which appeared from December 9, 1916, to February 3, 1917. The articles tell lesser-known facts about Oakley's career, especially her world travels. Some have never been published elsewhere. (No byline appears, so it's unclear if they were written by a staff reporter, a fan, or Oakley herself.) Although they are rife with hyperbole and purple prose—"She can out-shoot William Tell in her sleep and can drive nails with a Smith and Wesson revolver quite as rapidly as a steam hammer"—these articles provide valuable insights into Oakley's reception in Europe.

In the first installment of "Memories of Annie Oakley," she describes how the Wild West Show cast members were denied entrance into Russia because they were carrying firearms. Nothing they said to the officials could convince them they were using the guns in a performance. The Russians saw it as a threat and denied them access.

In another article, Oakley recalls that when French aristocrats saw Frank's gun, they invited him out for a friendly shooting competition. They were incredulous when Frank told them that Annie was a better shot and that she should be the one competing. Nevertheless, to keep things amicable, they invited the little missus along. Thinking they could make money from these American rubes, the aristocrats wagered $350 against Oakley. She doesn't tell us exactly what transpired; all she says is that she walked off with the $350.

Not all her memories of Europe were happy. She was shaken by the poverty she saw in Barcelona when the troupe spent Christmas there in 1891. Buffalo Bill decided to lower the admission cost of the show, and they collected $600 on their first night. Half was counterfeit. The cast tried to spend the cash in local stores, but the shopkeepers wouldn't take it, knowing that it was bogus. Smallpox and typhoid were also rampant in the city. Tragically, seven Native Americans from the Wild West Show died of typhoid during that trip to Barcelona.

Oakley recalled her trip to Austria with fondness. When the Baroness de Rothschild asked Oakley to give an exhibition for the orphans of Vienna, Oakley readily accepted. She played to a capacity audience and was thrilled to bring in much money for the orphans. As a gesture of gratitude, the Baroness gave Oakley a bag "full of gold pieces." Annie promptly donated it to the orphans.

Oakley also met Francis Joseph, emperor of Austria, who invited the Butlers to the historic palace of Schonbrunn. The emperor was eager to show off his country's military might. They toured the arsenal, which impressed Oakley. She deemed it "one of the most modern and complete in the world—but was at the same time a museum reaching back into the Middle Ages—an old curiosity shop of obsolete and primitive weapons of the Empire." Among the artifacts was a vast collection of bullets from around the world, which Annie admired. The emperor gave Oakley a selection of the best bullets, which she treasured all her life.

Perhaps the most charming story in the Memories of Annie Oakley series involved a fancy bracelet Annie often wore: a diamond-studded gold beauty with the name "Luitpold" engraved on it. When the interviewer asked Oakley how she came to own such an unusual piece, Annie told the following story.

The king of Bavaria, whom Annie deemed "one of the most unassuming and genuine men of all the royal folks I ever met," was a big fan. One afternoon, the king stopped by the camp to watch Oakley practice. Her skill captivated him, especially when she hit a dime out of the air. But as he intently watched her shoot, a bucking bronco charged. The king thought the horse posed no real threat, so he did not move. Recognizing the imminent danger, Oakley dropped her gun, ran to the king, and tackled him to the ground, saving his life. "I supposed I am the only person alive that ever knocked a ruling sovereign down and got away with it," she said. The next day, a courier from the palace arrived. He presented Oakley with the gorgeous gold bracelet.

As a performer, Oakley worked tirelessly to maintain her girl-like appearance, wearing her long brown hair loose down her back and her skirts relatively short. Newspapers often describe how she "tripped" and "skipped" on stage, like a young girl flirting with the audience. Late in her career, when her hair turned white prematurely, Oakley wore a brown wig during performances.

A pioneer in a male-dominated arena, Oakley fiercely guarded her public persona. While other female variety performers might be scantily clad, Oakley dressed in modest, ladylike costumes, which she often made herself (she was an accomplished seamstress and embroiderer). "To be considered a lady has always been my highest ambition," she once remarked. Oakley was careful never to cross the line of impropriety and would mock other women shooters who were provocative or unrefined. She did not wear makeup and refused to use tricks to enhance her shooting. Notoriously frugal, Oakley did not drink, smoke or cuss, although she might drink the occasional beer if someone else were buying. Her brother John once said, "She was pure in heart and spirit. I never heard her utter a cuss word in her life. She prayed on her knees every night." Fred Stone, a close friend, noted the following: "There was never a sweeter, gentler, more lovable woman than Annie Oakley. It was always amusing to watch people who were meeting her for the first time. They expected to see a big, masculine, blustering sort of person, and the tiny woman with the quiet voice took them by surprise."

As her biographer Glenda Riley notes, Oakley's strict adherence to ladylike decorum helped her to be accepted in a traditionally male sport. Perhaps her upbringing was also a factor, for Oakley believed the Quaker philosophy that women could make important contributions to society rather than merely reflect their husbands' glory.

Oakley fiercely guarded her image because she had prejudice to live down. She once wrote, "When I began shooting in public, it was considered almost shameful for a woman to shoot. This was a man's business, you see. Sometimes when I was invited to shoot at trap-shooting clubs, their wives and women friends of the members would be invited. They would look me over, ofttimes disdainfully, but I would not mind them at all."

It wasn't just men who balked at a woman shooter; women also disapproved. Women were often her most strident critics. And so, it's understandable that maintaining a sterling reputation was central to her success.

To Oakley, reputation was all important. That explains why she went to such lengths to sue newspapers when they printed false, defamatory stories about her. "Annie Oakley has an uncontrollable appetite for drugs," one headline screamed. "She steals to support her cocaine habit and is in a Chicago jail," said another. In response, Oakley sued the newspapers that printed the scurrilous material, winning all but one suit. She recouped $27,000. After paying the legal fees, however, Oakley ended up losing money. But it didn't matter. She had cleared her name.

Women at Pinehurst Gun Club. *Wilson Special Collections Library, UNC–Chapel Hill.*

Although she shattered gender barriers, Oakley did not support women's suffrage and dismissed the efforts of the New Woman. She disapproved of women wearing pants, also called bloomers. "There is nothing so detestable as a bloomer costume," she sniffed. Like many fascinating figures in history, Oakley was a bundle of contradictions. As one writer says, "She was provocative, appealing and reassuring, all at once." It should also be remembered that Oakley advocated for women in sports and to be self-employed at a time when such things were taboo.

Above all, Oakley wanted to be remembered for teaching thousands of women how to use firearms. She speaks with pride at having taught many "idle women" (her words) in Pinehurst how to shoot, and she believed that women should always have a gun by their bedside. She even published instructions on how to hide a pistol in one's parasol. Shooting, Oakley affirmed, was an athletic performance, one that would help a woman maintain her ladylike comportment:

> *I believe every woman should learn how to shoot. It would give them confidence and power of self-protection. And above all, it would teach them grace and poise. You cannot imagine how shooting demands perfect balance, and how shooting vanishes carelessness and slovenly ways. I know of nothing better in securing grace than practicing the poses which must be gone through in successfully handling a rifle or shotgun.*

One can only imagine what the leaders of the debutante ball thought of that.

DuPont Controversy

The Butlers' years in Pinehurst were not without controversy. Letters exchanged in 1920 between Leonard Tufts and E.R. Gavin from the DuPont Powder Company indicate that Frank Butler had been stirring up trouble. According to the letters, Frank claimed that Dead Shot Gun Powder would be used in Pinehurst instead of DuPont. Gavin wrote that company executives were stunned at the announcement, for DuPont powder had been used in Pinehurst for decades. Leonard Tufts was quick to set the matter straight.

In his letter to Gavin, Tufts clarified that Frank Butler did not speak on behalf of Tufts or his village. Pinehurst had no intention of switching

Tin of DuPont powder on display at Tufts Archives. *Photo by author.*

gunpowder. Gavin responded with evident relief and hinted at a probable reason for Frank's odd behavior.

When Oakley worked for Buffalo Bill's Wild West Show, the DuPont Company had "paid her a small monthly stipend," which they continued for many years afterward. But because of recent budget cuts, DuPont had ended the stipend. Frank seemed furious and was working out "his personal grudge" against the company. In the end, Tufts, ever the shrewd businessman, made it clear where his loyalty lay. When choosing between DuPont powder and the Frank Butlers, "Mr. and Mrs. B will have to go," he wrote to Gavin. The Butlers left Pinehurst two years later, never to return.

DESPITE HER INTERNATIONAL FAME, Oakley remained a private person in her later years. She did not like sobriquets like "champion of the world" but preferred to be considered simply an "exceptionally fine shot." While she acknowledged she had been blessed with unusual talent, she also stressed that this talent was honed through hours and hours of study and practice. When she was performing, she practiced every day. She was also highly disciplined with diet and exercise, retaining her slim figure and physical fitness all her life.

Oakley kept her charity work private, too. Her family noted that Annie did not spend her fortune on herself or "selfish and extravagant living" but lavished her family and friends with gifts. In 1920, the Butlers participated in a Pinehurst fundraiser to benefit the Farm Life School, selling her autographs for the school's benefit.

During World War I, the Butlers raised money for the Red Cross. They also traveled, at their own expense, to encampments across the country under the auspices of the National War Council of the YMCA. Oakley performed for an estimated half million troops. She later said that these exhibitions were more inspiring than the thousands of cheering crowds she enjoyed during her Wild West tours. During the war, Oakley wrote to Secretary of War Henry L. Stimson, offering to train and prepare a regiment

Annie Oakley in Pinehurst. *Wilson Special Collections Library, UNC–Chapel Hill.*

of women sharpshooters to protect the homeland. The offer was ignored.

In 1924, two years before she died, Oakley did a remarkable thing: she had *all* her gold medals melted down so she could give the proceeds to charity, including a hospital for tuberculosis patients in Montrose, North Carolina. (Two of her beloved sisters had died of the dreaded disease, and Annie never forgot their misery.) Historians say this collection of medals would be priceless today not only for their precious metal content but also for the peerless shooting records they represent. It was only after her death that it was discovered Oakley had anonymously paid for the education of at least twenty young women.

In 1922, the Butlers were in a severe car accident when their automobile flipped over an embankment. Frank was unhurt, but Annie fractured her hip and ankle. She would have to walk with a metal brace for the rest of her life. It was a tough blow for someone who had been active her whole life. Her friend Will Rogers visited after the accident and found her despondent. Thousands of fans sent cards, flowers, and well wishes. But Oakley never fully recovered. She passed away from pernicious anemia in 1926. Frank died three weeks later.

While Oakley enjoyed stardom and wealth earlier in her life, she spent her Pinehurst years in humanitarian giving. Oakley took deep satisfaction in knowing she had taught some fifteen thousand women (her estimate) to shoot in her lifetime. Such experience proved that, as she had always maintained, "individual for individual, women can shoot as well as men."

Chapter 5

THE WOMEN'S NORTH AND SOUTH

Golf is not an enemy to romance but it is a cure for romantic nonsense. Exercise and fresh air are sane remedies for silly infatuations.
—Glenna Collett (interview, 1928)

Golf historians tell us that women have been playing golf since the game's inception. Mary Queen of Scots, for instance, teed off on the fields of Seton in the sixteenth century. She kept a cottage in St. Andrews so she could play the game as often as possible, and it was she who first coined the word "caddie" from the French *cadet*. (Young military cadets evidently carried her clubs.) By the nineteenth century, golf was all the rage among women on both sides of the Atlantic. A ladies' golf club was formed at St. Andrews in Scotland in 1867 with five hundred members, and the Scottish Ladies' Golfing Association formed in 1903. The first U.S. women's championship occurred in 1895 at the Meadowbrook Club in Hampstead, New York. And so, it is no surprise that women played golf in Pinehurst from its earliest days, back when James Walker Tufts was worried about how errant golf balls were disturbing his cows' milk production.

While there have been many golfing greats to play and win in Pinehurst, from Babe Zaharias to Patty Berg to Minjee Lee, this chapter focuses on thirteen athletes who won the Women's North and South Amateur's Championship, a tournament played in Pinehurst since 1903 (the men's since 1901). Originally called the "North and South Open Championship Tournament," the North and South, as it's affectionately known, is so named

A poster of a Victorian lady golfer in Pinehurst. *Photo by author.*

because golfers would stop to play in Pinehurst when they headed south in the winter and then again when they headed back north in the summer. The prestigious tournament is by invitation—only the top amateur golfers get the go-ahead.

At the fin de siècle in America, few outdoor sports besides tennis and croquet were available to women. When golf became popular among the leisure class in the 1890s, women flocked to the links. After World War I, Americans were golf-mad. According to one estimate, by the 1920s, there were approximately two million male and female golfers in the United States. American fashion magazines from the time feature models wearing chic golf attire. Indeed, the cavalier lifestyle of the flapper was linked to leisure sports like golf. Unsurprisingly, the popularity of women's golf in America coincided with the loosening of feminine restrictions, both in dress and in behavior.

As the popularity of women's golf increased, sportswriters began to take notice. Reading about women golfers in old newspapers is a history lesson in itself. The earliest articles tend to focus on physical carriage, dress, and looks. For instance, one journalist describes a golfer as a "fine looking swinger," perhaps employing a double entendre, while another is "tall and willowy" and "the woman with the most sex appeal." It's hard to imagine journalists describing Ben Hogan in such terms. (Even today, some of the world's top women golfers have complained that journalists spend too much time talking about what they wear and not enough time on how they play the game.)

Some of the old newspaper accounts are downright amusing. One reporter, writing in 1920, gives his opinion on why women might want to play golf: they want to be fashionable, they have nothing else to do, they are after the money, and they love the sport. Indeed, women may have wanted to be trendy, they may have been bored, and they may have loved to golf. But surely, money was never a factor because there wasn't any. Not for women golfers, anyway.

As more women played golf and played it well, reporters stopped focusing on their looks and started writing about their skills. From its earliest days, the *Outlook* covered women's tournaments with the same enthusiasm and excitement as the men's, perhaps reflecting how seriously Pinehurst takes golf. In 1903, the year of the women's first tournament, large photographs of winners of both sexes graced the front page.

By 1905, the women's North and South is described in the *Outlook* as "the most brilliant and hotly contested event in the history of the tournaments." Several hundred spectators closely watched "the tournament of surprises."

Top: A lady golfer in Pinehurst. *Wilson Special Collections Library, UNC–Chapel Hill.*
Bottom: A women's golf tournament. *Wilson Special Collections Library, UNC–Chapel Hill.*

A lady golfer in Pinehurst. *Moore County Historical Association.*

By 1917, reporters noted that all the top female competitors had loyal followers. And by the 1920s, the heyday of superstar Glenna Collett, women's tournaments drew massive crowds in Pinehurst, sometimes more than the men's. One gallery for the women's North and South was estimated at more than fifteen thousand. A nation that had become golf-mad had embraced its female competitors.

While many books have been devoted to the history of men's golf in Pinehurst (the Tufts Archives are filled with a disproportionate amount of memorabilia and artifacts celebrating men's golf), relatively little has been written about women golfers. So, it seemed fitting to include a chapter on women golfers who dazzled Pinehurst with their skill.

For convenience, I profile thirteen golfers who won the women's North and South from 1903 to 1948. The dates in parentheses indicate the year or years the golfer won the championship, and their names appear as they did on the official tournament roster. (It should be noted that these are brief snapshots of some golfing greats, not comprehensive biographies.)

Only two women in this chapter, Babe Didrikson Zaharias and Louise Suggs, were original founders of the Ladies Professional Golf Association (LPGA). By all accounts, the turning point in women's golf came in 1950 with the establishment of the LPGA. Thirteen women worked tirelessly to establish a tournament schedule, secure radio and television coverage,

A lady golfer in Pinehurst. *Wilson Special Collections Library, UNC–Chapel Hill.*

and participate in the endless promotions necessary to advance women's golf. By the third season, more and more tournaments had been added, and prize money steadily increased. By its tenth year, the LPGA had grown from fourteen to twenty-six events and had quadrupled its total prize money. Much of what women professional golfers enjoy today is owed to these pioneers. To honor these pioneers, the front cover of this book features several founders of the LPGA standing in front of the iconic veranda of the Pinehurst Country Club.

MYRA PATERSON ('03, '05, '06)

New York native Myra Paterson (alternately spelled "Patterson") initially came to Pinehurst in 1899 to convalesce from the effects of early-stage tuberculosis. She often practiced her game on Pinehurst No. 1 when there was only one course in the village. So, it is no surprise that when Pinehurst sponsored its first women's North and South Amateur tournament, Paterson came out on top, competing against seventeen contestants. She won by fifteen strokes.

Myra Paterson. *Tufts Archives.*

Looking at photographs of Victorian-era golfers like Paterson, it's a
wonder that the women could even hit the ball, let alone win a major
tournament. Fashion at the time dictated that women show off their tiny
waists—eighteen inches was the ideal—including lady golfers. So many
golfers still wore corsets. They also wore heavy petticoats under floor-

length skirts and long-sleeved shirts with high collars, which were held in place by stiff stays. One newspaper account describes how a woman's neck would be rubbed raw after a long day on the links because of these rigid collars.

Victorian apparel was hardly conducive to playing sports, so women devised ingenious contrivances, like the "Miss Higgins." To cope with their long skirts billowing up in a strong wind, lady golfers would tie a large elastic band around their waist, which they affectionately called "Miss Higgins." Should a stiff breeze blow, the woman would slide Miss Higgins down to their ankles so that they could putt in peace. One spectator said that seeing these women out on the greens made it look like they were "encasing their bodies like sausages." Needs must. Paterson caused quite a sensation in Pinehurst when she played her rounds wearing a scandalous skirt eight inches off the ground.

Early women golfers routinely had their husbands or boyfriends caddie for them. Less often, they would hire a golf professional. In the earliest tournaments, women had no purse money, so they had to be satisfied with a silver cup and their photo in the paper. Despite the lack of remuneration, early golfers like Paterson played up and down the East Coast in whatever amateur tournaments they could find.

Paterson played golf into her seventies. She liked to rub elbows with the upper crust: in a 1909 Pinehurst Society column, Paterson is listed as a dinner guest of the famous bandleader John Philip Sousa. Not only was she an outstanding golfer, Paterson was also a strong advocate for women's golf. From 1910 to 1932, she was the first president of the Women's Metropolitan Golf Association, a precursor to the LPGA. She was an active member of the U.S. Seniors Association, recalling that "when we started the 'Seniors,' in 1924, we were afraid no woman would admit to being 45, but later we had to change the age minimum to 50. The women in their 40s were too good for us."

DOROTHY CAMPBELL HURD ('18, '20, '21)

Scottish sensation Dorothy Campbell Hurd took Pinehurst by storm in the early decades of the twentieth century. A large photograph of the talented golfer—dressed in tweeds and striking a confident swing—graces the front page of a 1918 *Outlook*. The article says that Campbell Hurd won the St. Valentine's Golf tournament in "masterful style."

Dorothy Campbell Hurd.
Wikimedia Commons.

Players like Campbell Hurd, who dominated women's golf on both sides of the Atlantic, could generate massive crowds. In 1909, the Scotland native won three major championships: the British, United States, and Canadian Opens. When she played in the women's tournament at St. Andrews, winning in 1910 and 1911, some nine thousand spectators turned out to see her play. Her 1921 North and South victory was hard won, for the playing field had deepened. Campbell Hurd faced stiff competition against the likes of golfing sensation Glenna Collett.

Campbell Hurd was not much of a driver but was known as a master of the greens. She was cool under pressure. Sportswriters of the day attest to her "brilliant golf," her "phenomenal accuracy" and her "calm at crucial moments." Watching Campbell Hurd play during one of the semifinal rounds of the 1918 women's North and South, one reporter from the *Outlook* gushed, "That was probably the best golf ever seen played by a woman on this course." According to one witness, Dorothy won the tournament, which was filled with "exciting rounds with many surprises." Another reporter described her remarkably smooth eleven-foot putt: "She put that in as if with a pen dropper." The simile is lost on modern readers until one realizes that fountain pens were filled with eye droppers, which would take precise eye-hand coordination. Campbell Hurd won an estimated 750 victories in her international career.

NONNA BARLOW ('15, '16, '19)

Anyone who has researched women of the Progressive era in America, whether writers, performers, or sports figures, knows that one of the challenges is identifying the woman's first name. Such is the case for Mrs. Ronald H. Barlow (alternately Mrs. *Roland* H. Barlow), who, although a championship golfer, is referred to in the Pinehurst paper only by her married name, a popular convention of the time. But Nonna Barlow won three North and South tournaments and several other large cups on the East Coast. From all accounts, the 1916 tournament was a nail-biter: "Not once during the contest was she more than a hair's breadth in the lead of any of her opponents." Born in Ireland, Barlow said she especially enjoyed playing in the Sandhills: "Pinehurst requires a real knowledge of the finesse of golf. If I can play there, I know I can play anywhere. If I win there, it puts me on the top of confidence for the rest of the season."

Nonna Barlow. *Wikimedia Commons.*

GLENNA COLLETT
('22, '23, '24, '27, '29, '30)

No American woman golfer dominated the sport in the 1920s like Glenna Collett. She drew enormous crowds whenever she played, and her fans followed her devotedly. Headlines from 1928 rely on superlatives: "[Collett] is the greatest woman golfer in the country at the present time" and "has smashed all records of women's golf in America." When a headline from a 1928 article read, "Glenna Shoots a 73 over Pine Needles Course," no one wonders which Glenna they meant.

A press favorite, Collett was arguably the sport's first female star. She was considered to be "remarkably pretty," according to the *Outlook*, having charisma and flair, but it was Glenna's game that people came to see. And they were never disappointed.

It's an understatement to say Collett was a gifted athlete. The Providence, Rhode Island native was the star of her brother's baseball team until her outraged mother forced her to quit and take up a "more genteel" sport like tennis or golf. Glenna was also a champion swimmer, diver, tennis player, and accomplished driver, reportedly teaching herself how to drive a car when she was ten.

Collett picked up golf at fourteen and was winning national championships five years later. Her father, George Collett, recognized his daughter's talent and hired pro golfer Alex Smith to coach Glenna when she was still in high school.

Glenna Collett. *Wikimedia Commons.*

During those formative years, Collett spent parts of each winter in Pinehurst learning how to perfect her game. She would make annual trips to Pinehurst for the next fifteen years.

Glenna revolutionized the way women played golf. A fellow competitor remarked, "Her vigorous attacking game set up an entirely fresh standard for her countrymen." Collett was a powerhouse. When she won the U.S. Women's Amateur Championship in 1922, she consistently outdrove her competition by 50 yards. She reportedly drove a ball 307 yards when she was just eighteen years old.

In addition to winning the North and South six times, she also won the U.S. Women's Amateur Championship six times. Routinely compared to Bob Jones, who dominated men's golf around the same time, Collett became nationally famous, even in "non-golfing households." However, Collett was not above throwing clubs when things didn't go her way. She was known for her temper.

At the height of her success in the '20s, Collett wintered in Pinehurst, bringing an entourage with her. After her big wins in 1922, the press reported that "public interest in all things Glenna rose to a fever pitch." In 1924, she won eleven out of the twelve tournaments she entered.

Collett took a break from the sport for two years (1933–35) after giving birth to two children. But she made a spectacular return in 1935, trouncing seventeen-year-old sensation Patty Berg. An estimated fifteen thousand spectators turned out for the event.

That would be Collett's last national tournament, although she played in regional competitions from time to time. In later years, she took up other sports like rifle shooting, winning several titles in her hometown of Philadelphia. When she and her husband, Edwin Vare, visited Pinehurst, they often played a round of golf, but they also enjoyed skeet shooting. Remarkably, when Collett was eighty years old, she played and won an exhibition match at St. Andrews. Often called the "Queen of the Links," Collett served on USGA committees for fifty years and was inducted into the Women's Golf Hall of Fame in 1950 and Pinehurst's World Golf Hall of Fame in 1975.

MAUREEN ORCUTT
('31, '32, '33; SENIORS '60, '61, '62)

Imagine playing a tough round of competitive golf and then having to slip back to the hotel to churn out copy for the *New York Times* sports page before tomorrow's deadline. That was the life for Maureen Orcutt, a six-time winner of the North and South, golf's grand "Duchess."

When she started writing for the Gray Lady, about fifty sportswriters were on staff, and only one female—Maureen Orcutt. She worked at the *Times* from 1937 to 1972. She didn't get a byline if she wrote about a tournament she was playing in. And if she made it to the finals, it was up to someone else to provide coverage. After all, Orcutt had to focus on her game. One of her fellow sportswriters said, "Maureen always made you feel happy. She was a kind person and just plain fun to be with. She was one of the folks who made our sports department in those days a wonderful place to work."

Some think that Orcutt was given the nickname "Duchess" because she hailed from Manhattan's Park Avenue (she did). Some say she was so called because she was active in the sport until ninety-two, when her knees finally gave out (again, true). But Orcutt was given the moniker by her coworkers at the *Times*, who considered her a good golfer and writer but an even better person. They called her "Duchess" as a term of endearment. Few in the history of ladies' golf were better liked than Maureen Orcutt.

Orcutt's introduction to golf is the stuff of legends. As a teen, she watched her parents play a few rounds and started criticizing her mother, as teenage daughters are wont to do. "Well, if you think you can do better," her mother said in exasperation, "then you can have my membership." Maureen grabbed her father's clubs and proceeded to trounce her mother. Mrs. Orcutt relinquished her membership. By the late 1920s, Orcutt would dominate women's golf, winning the U.S. Women's Amateur Championship in 1927, 1928 and 1930, becoming the first player to win the prestigious tournament three times.

Orcutt first visited Pinehurst in 1931. She found the place small, her accommodation in a private home uninspiring. For later tournaments, Orcutt preferred to stay at the Holly Inn with her mother, her biggest fan and traveling companion. They had a much better time at the inn, where folks would gather in the evenings to relax and play cards. It was the first time she had played on sand greens, and she recalls how a grounds crew member would come out with a carpet to smooth out the sand after a

Maureen Orcutt. *Tufts Archives.*

player was done putting. She also recalled that the caddies were exceptional at Pinehurst because they knew the contours of the course intimately.

While her first tournaments were played on No. 3, Orcutt did play—and win—on No. 2: "I loved to play Pinehurst No 2. I could *hit* the ball. I used to be a *hitter*, they'd say, and I loved to let out, and you could let out on No. 2." Indeed, many consider Orcutt one of the game's best long-iron female players of the time.

Sources differ regarding her number of career wins: sixty-four, sixty-five or sixty-eight. But whatever the number, Orcutt had an impressive career. She is one of few golfers who can claim that they won at Pinehurst on sand greens ('31, '32, '33) and grass greens ('60, '61, '62). Orcutt, who is in the World Golf Hall of Fame, was still winning club titles well into her eighties. Known for her big, toothy smile, a Pinehurst reporter once wrote, "Maureen Orcutt is a colorful personality....In any competition the crowd is with her because she always comes through from the most difficult situation to a flying finish."

ESTELLE LAWSON PAGE
('35, '37, '39, '40, '41, '44, '45)

Estelle Lawson Page holds the record for the most wins of the women's North and South—seven. And she had her father to thank for it.

Estelle was an average tennis player at UNC–Chapel Hill when her father, Dr. Robert Lawson, encouraged her to pick up golf instead. It was a fortuitous decision, for Estelle would win more than seven hundred trophies throughout her career. An orthopedic surgeon, her father served as her first and only coach. As he tutored his daughter, he explained what muscles and bones were involved in each swing and putt.

Observers said that Estelle had a natural swing, and many were amazed that she never had any formal lessons. She hadn't played on any major circuit before she won her first championship—the U.S. Nationals, beating Patty Berg.

A newspaper account of her first round of competition in Pinehurst notes that "she hurried back to Chapel Hill following her round to cook dinner for her husband, Julius." A full-page spread depicts a caricature of Lawson Page's career. In one frame, she is fiercely eyeing the National Championship. In the next, she has donned an apron and is running to bring her husband a hot meal. In the last frame, she is hitting a golf ball. The article announces that Lawson Page cannot play the winter tour "because of her household duties."

A newspaper account from 1945 covers Lawson Page's win at the North and South but also mentions her husband, Staff Sergeant Julius Page, who was seriously wounded in France and Germany during World War

Estelle Lawson Page (*left*) and Peggy Kirk Bell. *Tufts Archives.*

II. While he was recouping in a British hospital, a fellow soldier in the next bed asked if he was related to Mrs. Page, "the good golfer." Julius was proud to say that yes, he was.

LOUISE SUGGS ('42, '46, '48)

Quiet. A loner. One of golf's quiet people. Such were the words used to describe a legend of American golf, Louise Suggs. Known for her smooth swing and steely concentration, Suggs played with quiet intensity. She was the antithesis of her contemporary, the exuberant "Babe" Zaharias, her rival for many tournaments.

Suggs grew up in a golfing household. The Georgia native started playing golf on a course designed and built by her father. Suggs was the first woman to beat male professionals on a head-to-head basis. She was a founding

Louise Suggs. *Wikimedia Commons.*

member of the LPGA and its president from 1955 to 1957. In 1948, Suggs turned professional and won sixty-one professional tournaments, including eleven majors. Inducted into the World Golf Hall of Fame and the LPGA Hall of Fame, Suggs was one of the first women golfers to win lucrative contracts with top sporting manufacturers. She was the league's leading money winner in 1953 and 1960. In 1957, Suggs achieved the career Grand Slam, winning all major tournaments for women.

Despite her reserve, Suggs was a generous mentor and teacher and an outspoken advocate for equal recognition and prize money for women. Suggs recognized she was on the cusp of seismic changes in women's pro golf. "I believe I may have arrived twenty years too soon," Suggs noted, "but the day is dawning for women golfers."

MILDRED "BABE" DIDRIKSON ZAHARIAS ('47)

Three-time Olympic medalist (1932), Major League Baseball pitcher, vaudeville performer, music recording star, film star for RKO, championship golfer, and founding member of the LPGA, Mildred "Babe" Didrikson Zaharias is considered the greatest female athlete of all time. Some say the greatest athlete, period. Babe was an All-American in track and field and basketball but also excelled at baseball, diving, bowling, and anything that was remotely competitive. She even won sewing competitions back in her home state of Texas. Childhood friends recall that when she was just twelve, Babe (a nickname given to her by her family from childhood) declared she wanted to be "the greatest athlete that ever lived." It was a self-fulfilling prophecy. People who have never seen photos of Zaharias assume she was husky and broad-shouldered, but Babe was slim (126 pounds) and slightly above average height (five feet, seven inches). What set her apart was her natural athleticism and competitive drive.

Babe was twenty-four when she started playing golf and was already a celebrity on this side of the Atlantic because of her Olympic wins and the RKO shorts. Although she was not above embellishing a story for self-promotion, Zaharias insists that the first time she picked up a golf club, she drove the balls 240 to 260 yards, outshooting all the men she was playing with. But Zaharias didn't just show up on the greens one day and start winning tournaments. She spent twelve to sixteen hours a day practicing. Babe was considered a professional athlete at the time, so she was barred from amateur golf until 1940, when her amateur status was reinstated.

In 1946, Zaharias won seventeen straight golf tournaments—in one year! In 1950, she won the Grand Slam of golf: the U.S. Open, the Titleholders Championship, and the Women's Western Open. She was the first American to win the British Ladies Championship and the league's leading money winner. According to her friend Patty Berg, Babe changed how women played golf. "Until she came along," Berg said, "women were all swing and no hit. Babe swung, but she also hit. She put power into the women's game."

While not all her peers loved Babe (Louise Suggs, for one, despised her antics), the gallery adored her. Zaharias loved to clown around after making great shots and would often "wisecrack with the galleries," as she put it. She was known for her colorful personality and humor. "It's not enough just to swing at the ball," Babe said. "You've got to loosen your girdle and really let the ball have it."

Babe Zaharias. *Wikimedia Commons.*

From her years in entertainment, Zaharias knew how to play to the crowd. Photos of her from the '30s and '40s invariably show a smiling Babe, mugging for the camera, doing (or saying) something outrageous. She once posed on the roof of a car for publicity. The press loved her because nothing sold copy like a photo of Babe doing something outlandish. But close friends say that there was something more behind the clown persona.

Since its beginning, golf in America has always been associated with the moneyed leisure class, and women golfers were no exception. Lady golfers were expected to look and dress according to feminine dictates, for golf was considered a more feminine sport than, say, baseball. Enter Babe Didrikson: a wiry, muscular woman with a plain face and brash manners who craved the limelight and was not above telling a blue joke. According to those close to her, Babe had to put up with "snubs and slights and the downright venom of a lot of women" in golfing circles. Some even tried to prevent her from playing because she didn't fit the mold of the suave, elegant golfer.

Love her or hate her, no one would deny that Babe was the face of the LPGA and perhaps the single biggest reason for its success. It was precisely her outgoing personality that the fledgling LPGA needed. Babe turned professional in 1947 and was the public persona behind the LPGA.

It's hard to overstate how important Zaharias was to women's golf. As one of the founding members of the LPGA, Zaharias worked tirelessly to champion women's golf, attending photo shoots, making speeches, and posing with sponsors. Many of her contemporaries have said that the LPGA would not have been established if it hadn't been for Babe. Close friend and golfing peer Peggy Kirk Bell said that Babe recognized the social aspect of the sport and was especially proud of her golfing successes.

The Babe won eighty-two tournaments throughout her golfing career and was inducted into the LPGA Hall of Fame in 1951. In 1953, four months after being treated for colon cancer, Zaharias won the U.S. Women's Open while wearing a colostomy bag. In 1954, she was voted Woman Athlete of the Year by the Associated Press for the sixth time.

Peggy Kirk Bell ('49)

Peggy Kirk Bell's initiation to Pinehurst reads like a work of fiction. A teenager at Rollins College in Florida who played on the golf team, Peggy Kirk drove up from the Sunshine State and arrived in Pinehurst a day before the tournament. The college co-ed was immediately star-struck by the "famous golf capital of the world," as she saw it. When she went into the clubhouse to pay her entry fee, the man behind the desk asked for her invitation. "What invitation?" she naively asked. So green was she that Kirk Bell did not know the tournament was by invitation only. Luckily, Richard Tufts was on hand to rectify the situation. Peggy was given an official invitation and was able to enter the contest. But, as she liked to say, on her inaugural visit to Pinehurst, she "crashed the party." She won the tournament.

Though she would eventually settle in the Sandhills, the Ohio native was initially awestruck by Pinehurst's smart set. She noted how the people were "sort of classy.…People that played golf dressed in very handsome clothes

Peggy Kirk Bell (*left*) and Babe Zaharias. *Moore County Historical Association.*

and I remember seeing the men in the brown and white wing tips…things you did not see at other clubs." Even at the local theater, people dressed to the nines. "The ladies would have on long evening gowns and the men would have on their tuxedos," she noted.

Kirk Bell won the North and South in 1949, the first year the women played on Pinehurst No. 2. "I told them I'd have to get on that big course and then I'd prove I could play," she said. She was on the winning team for the United States for the Curtis Cup in 1950, but she never played professionally.

Around Pinehurst, Kirk Bell is remembered for her teaching and advocacy. You don't have to live in the Sandhills long to know that the name "Peggy Kirk Bell" is sacrosanct. Her reputation as an educator is second to none, and some say that no one did more for women's golf than Peggy Kirk Bell.

In 1953, with her husband, Warren "Bullet" Bell, Peggy bought Pine Needles Lodge and Golf Club in Southern Pines, with a course designed by Donald Ross. (For lodging, they initially had to use army barracks left over from World War II.) Pine Needles was where Peggy started her career as a golf instructor.

The story goes that a woman had come into the golf shop for lessons. The Bells didn't employ an instructor at the time, so Warren looked over at his wife and told her to get to it. Even though she knew nothing about teaching, Peggy knew a lot about golf. So she jumped in. As Peggy recalls, she overwhelmed the woman with a boatload of instruction and wouldn't be surprised if her first student quit golf altogether. But something clicked, and Peggy's career in golf instruction was launched.

Kirk Bell was close friends with Babe Zaharias, recalling how Babe did not know how to turn off the competitive switch. Even when ironing clothes, Babe would brag that she was the best ironer in the world, Peggy recalls. At the same time, she quickly points out how kindhearted Zaharias was. Few people knew how much Babe helped other cancer patients when she was dying from the disease. "She loved people. She loved life more than anyone else I can think of," Peggy recalls.

For more than sixty years, Peggy Kirk Bell was the lead instructor at the Pine Needles, developing her "Golfari" instructional program. In 2019, in the lifetime achievement category, she was inducted into the World Golf Hall of Fame. In 1990, she was given the Bob Jones Award, the highest honor the USGA gave in recognition of distinguished sportsmanship in golf. In 2002, she became the first woman voted into the World Golf Teachers Hall of Fame. ESPN once described Kirk Bell as "the premier advocate for women's golf."

Even though she enjoyed playing the game, teaching was her first love: "It has been my life....I look forward to teaching every day."

Chapter 6

Jalopy Soccer and Pig Races

While Pinehurst is known as the "cradle of American golf," boasting nineteen courses and counting, the village was once home to an active sports scene that didn't involve clubs, greens, and little white balls. Under the 1928 masthead of the *Pinehurst Outlook*, one reads: "golf, hunting, field trials, archery, riding, polo, trapshooting, fox hunts, horseracing, tennis." Indeed, reading through archival materials from the 1920s and '30s, one gets the sense that with the demise of its founder, Pinehurst shed its Puritanical garb and adopted a zanier form of entertainment. Forget the formal attire and martinis on the veranda. Folks were mad for jalopy soccer, pig races, and that newest craze—miniature golf.

THISTLE DHU

While most people think that the first miniature golf course in the United States was located behind one of James Barber's houses, Thistle Dhu, in Pinehurst village, that is only partly correct. The first miniature golf course, called Lilliputian, was actually situated behind another of Barber's Pinehurst homes, Cedarcrest, and not the Thistle Dhu mansion. The Lilliputian (named after the miniature people in *Gulliver's Travels*) was a nine-hole miniature golf course built in 1916. It was designed as a form of entertainment for Barber's guests. When his newer, grander home was completed in 1919, Barber commissioned Edward H. Wiswell to design an eighteen-hole miniature

Jalopy soccer at Sandhills fairgrounds. *Tufts Archives.*

golf course on the grounds. Legend has it that when Barber surveyed the completed miniature golf course behind his new property, he responded in characteristic understatement: "This'll do." The name stuck, albeit with a Scottish twist—Thistle Dhu.

Initially described as an eighteen-hole putting course, Thistle Dhu lacked windmills, drawbridges, or castles. It was, quite simply, a beautiful golf course in miniature. Wiswell, a golfing enthusiast and amateur architect, designed each hole to be unique, using the natural surroundings as equal parts decoration and hazard. The course was notoriously tricky, with elevated greens surrounded by a maze of shrubbery and flower beds. In the center was a fountain. One experienced player called it a "golfing nightmare" and "the world's craziest, most scientific and most aggravating golf course." Glenna Collett pronounced it a "lovely course."

Wiswell penned an article about the course for the August 1919 edition of *Popular Science*, in which he described each hole in detail. The following year, Barber's backyard course was featured in the British magazine *Country Life*, where the author wrote, "It was built for the hard thinker rather than the hard hitter." Two feature articles in national magazines contributed to the fame of Barber's miniature golf course.

Guests who wanted to play a round at Thistle Dhu were charged fifty cents, which included admission to the course, a glass of lemonade, and

Pig racing at the Carolina Hotel. *Moore County Historical Association.*

Thistle Dhu, Barber's house in Pinehurst. *Wilson Special Collections Library, UNC–Chapel Hill.*

Miniature golf course behind Barber's house. *Tufts Archives.*

some sandwiches. Proceeds went to the Farm Life School in Aberdeen. Occasionally, Barber would hold tournaments. An announcement in the *Pinehurst Outlook*, dated April 14, 1920, gives the winner's name out of a field of fifty golfers. Some thought winning Thistle Dhu was as good as cinching the North and South.

James Barber was president of the Barber Steamship Company, a worldwide maritime transportation company. Barber, his wife, Kate, and their seven children lived in Pinehurst from 1912 until his death in 1928. Barber was an active member of the Tin Whistles and was influential in the Sandhills, one of the leading financial partners behind Knollwood Corporation. According to one source, Barber owned a "small empire" in the Sandhills. Barber was also a philanthropist and played a key role in building the Village Chapel.

Mr. and Mrs. Michael Meehan purchased the home from the Barber family, donating it in 1947 to the Catholic Diocese of Raleigh when the building was renamed Maryhurst Retreat House. Currently, the house and grounds are in private hands. Although the Thistle Dhu name remains, almost nothing is left of the original miniature golf course. In 2012, a seventeen-thousand-foot putting course was opened at Pinehurst Resort and Country Club. Its name? Thistle Dhu.

GYMKHANAS

Gymkhanas, imported from England and popular in the early decades of the twentieth century, were outdoor activities involving all sorts of games and races for recreational purposes. They were all the rage in Pinehurst, especially in the '20s and '30s. Gymkhanas were madcap fun. There were donut races, clothespin races, and half-mile races on donkeys. There were walk and canter competitions and potato wars, where competitors speared as many potatoes as possible with a long stick and dropped them into a barrel guarded by a somber judge. While these were deemed "harmless frolics" in the *Outlook*, some events were dangerous. Grabbing a ring at full gallop, throwing apples through a hoop at full gallop, and tearing a ribbon off your competitor at, you guessed it, full gallop was not for the faint of heart. If comedy was more to your liking, you could enter the cross-dressing race: women dressed in men's attire and men dressed as women and then raced one another. In typical hyperbole, a reporter for the *Outlook* writes the following about gymkhanas: "No affairs of the season are more universally enjoyed by the entire colony; no season would be complete without them."

Potato race at Sandhills Fairgrounds. *Tufts Archives.*

Broom polo at Sandhills Fairgrounds. *Tufts Archives.*

Grandstand at Sandhills Fairgrounds. *Wilson Special Collections Library, UNC–Chapel Hill.*

Gymkhana at the Carolina Hotel. *Wilson Special Collections Library, UNC–Chapel Hill.*

Judging cows at Sandhills Fairgrounds. *Wilson Special Collections Library, UNC–Chapel Hill.*

Pageant at Sandhills Fairgrounds. *Wilson Special Collections Library, UNC–Chapel Hill.*

Aerial view of Sandhills Racetrack. *Wilson Special Collections Library, UNC–Chapel Hill.*

Weekly gymkhanas occurred at the Harness Racetrack or the Carolina Hotel, where afternoon tea and musical entertainment followed. Historic photos show adult riders alongside children and older folks. Some events, like the steeplechase, were serious, but most were "foolish or amusing" like broom polo, horse soccer, mule polo, obstacle courses, and jalopy soccer. During the holiday season, one could participate in a tilting contest, a roping-the-goat contest, or a turkey race. For the kids, there were spoon-and-egg races along with the traditional wheelbarrow or three-legged race. There was even something called "musical stalls." Riders would prance in and out of horse stalls set up on the polo field as Christmas music filtered through the loudspeakers. When the music stopped, the rider who remained outside a stall was out of the contest. They don't call it the leisure class for nothing.

Besides the contests, there were displays and pageants of all kinds, including local beauty contests and livestock competitions. A 1940 article announces another curious display: "Little Squire, the jumping equine marvel," would appear at the Carolina Hotel gymkhana, an event not to be missed. Pinehurst had its very own Li'l Sebastian.

Archery

By the turn of the century, archery had begun taking hold in resort towns like Pinehurst. While most archers played outdoors in vacant fields, in the 1920s and 1930s, there was a movement in the United States to bring archery into the workplace. The exercise and competition were believed to help fuel hard work and enterprise. One reads of indoor ranges in long corridors of office buildings and factories—hopefully, no one stuck their head out of their office at the wrong time. An article touting the benefits of indoor archery suggests that management should get on board, for "it is a well-established fact that a good archer almost invariably is well above the average in his vocation." At the same time, archery was touted as a health-giving exercise. A brochure from the 1920s reads, "Doctors recommend—and practice—Archery as an ideal exercise to broaden shoulders, steady the eye, hand and nerve."

According to announcements in the *Outlook*, archery was being added to the Pinehurst resort as early as 1909. By 1926, the Pinehurst Archery Club had opened its doors. While the sport appealed primarily to women, men also participated. The archery club was located a few blocks from the Carolina Hotel and was overseen by Philip and Elizabeth Rounsevelle.

Above: Women's archery in Pinehurst. *Tufts Archives.*

Left: Archery in Pinehurst. *Moore County Historical Association.*

The Rounsevelles moved from New Orleans to open the Archers Company, which made and sold customized bows, arrows and everything related to archery. They moved their headquarters to Pinehurst because of the warm climate and "the type of people who live in the Sandhills and who come here as tourists." In other words, the sporty set. Elizabeth was a nationally ranked archer who gave lessons, and Philip oversaw production. According to an advertisement, the company was home to the famous "Pinehurst patented fire-back bow" made from Norwegian pine.

In 1926 (some sources say January 1927), Pinehurst hosted the first Annual Midwinter archery tournament, which attracted archers from around the country. After that, the match was typically held in March and spanned three to five days. Golf star Glenna Collett was an accomplished archer who always attracted large crowds. Indeed, archery was a fan favorite. An article from 1929 announces that "the rifle and the archery ranges are still going at full blast, each drawing its group of interested participants." In inclement weather, the Carolina Hotel might set up a miniature range for guests in their ballroom.

Pinehurst is reportedly home to the country's first miniature archery-golf course. A hybrid of golf and archery, the amalgamation was played in Pinehurst as early as 1927. In 1933, nine unused holes on Pinehurst No. 5 became home to Pinehurst's first official archery-golf course. Donald Ross was an enthusiastic supporter of the sport. Historians tell us that archery-golf is not new but that a form of the sport, Rovers, was played in merry England during the Middle Ages.

In Pinehurst and throughout the country, the popularity of archery hit its zenith during the Roaring Twenties. Advertisements from the time call Pinehurst "the American Archery Center." By 1932, Pinehurst had hired national champion Russ Hooggerhyde to serve as an instructor at the club. But by the mid-1930s, perhaps due to the Great Depression, the Archers Company closed its doors for good. The building was sold in 1937 and turned into a nightclub.

ROQUE

One of the more popular games in Pinehurst was roque (pronounced "rock"), the American form of croquet. Like its English cousin, roque uses a mallet, wickets, and hard ball. But roque is played on a hard, smooth surface rather than a grass lawn, and the wickets are permanently anchored in place. The mallet sticks are shorter, and the rules of the game differ. A low wall encircles the court in roque, so one can hit the ball off the sides to make a play. Advertisements in Boston newspapers from 1863 announce roque competitions. Roque was also popular at the turn of the century and was even a sport at the 1904 Summer Olympics. The American Roque League was founded in 1916, lasting until the 1950s, when it was overshadowed and replaced by the more popular croquet.

Many believe that James Walker Tufts introduced the sport to Pinehurst. Announcements in the *Outlook* from 1904 and 1905 attest to the sport's popularity. New roque courts were added in 1907, and by 1911, there were numerous places in the village where people could go to play. By the late 1920s, roque games seemed to have gravitated to Southern Pines. Interest in Pinehurst eventually died out.

Croquet was also played in Pinehurst from its inception. Men and women, young and old, could play, making it one of the few sports the whole family could enjoy. Croquet sets were affordable, and families could play on their front lawns. By 1865, croquet clubs were forming in the Northeast, and public grounds were opened throughout the country. An 1863 article in a Boston newspaper calls croquet "the rage of the summer." As with any competitive sport, tempers flared. A Boston newspaper article describes a death by croquet mallet—an incensed player hit another over the head with a mallet, causing his demise.

With so many of Pinehurst's visitors coming from the Northeast, it is no wonder the game would find its way to the Sandhills. Croquet is mentioned as early as 1897 in the *Pinehurst Outlook*. Today, Pinehurst is an epicenter for the sport, boasting "three of the nation's largest international and regulation courts."

TENNIS

By 1895, tennis ranked as the top outdoor sport in the country, and Pinehurst accommodated its tennis players. The original village had six clay tennis courts and organized many tournaments. In 1903, in response to demands from guests, Pinehurst organized six tournaments, including men's and women's singles and mixed doubles. The entrance fee was twenty-five cents. New tennis courts were built in front of the resort.

Capitalizing on the brand familiarity of the North and South golf tournament, Pinehurst hosted its first North and South Championship Tournament for tennis in 1919, which attracted top players from around

Tennis at Pinehurst Country Club. *Moore County Historical Association.*

the country. The village hired its first tennis professional in 1927, and by 1938, the North and South tennis tournament had become a professional tournament, drawing Wimbledon, Olympic, and national title holders. Local matches were also popular.

In addition to courts at the country club, the Carolina Hotel and the Holly Inn also had tennis courts for guests. Pinehurst hosted the Annual Mid-Winter Tennis Championship, which naturally appealed to northerners who could not play their beloved sport outdoors in the winter. In the 1970s, there was a surge of interest in the sport; Pinehurst responded by building twenty-four courts and a tennis complex.

POLO

The rise of polo in Pinehurst mirrors the rise of the sport nationwide. Even though the United States Polo Association (USPA) was created in 1890, the sport did not gain traction until the Roaring Twenties. By the 1930s, crowds of more than thirty thousand gathered to watch polo matches on Long Island in New York. The Sandhills Polo Club, created in 1920, was the brainchild of Captain A. Loftus Bryan of the British army. He was the driving force behind the club, acting as its first player and coach. Within a year, an indoor practice ring for polo was being constructed behind the Carolina Hotel. Walter Slocock eventually took the club's reins

Polo players in Pinehurst. *Moore County Historical Association.*

Polo at Pinehurst Racetrack. *Wilson Special Collections Library, UNC–Chapel Hill.*

Will Rogers (*center*) playing polo in Pinehurst. *Tufts Archives.*

and helped establish the program in the Sandhills. By 1928, polo was a top sport in Pinehurst.

The Sandhills Polo Club hosted club and major tournaments, including the Intercollegiate Polo Championship. They often squared off with the Fort Bragg Whites, a polo team from the nearby army base (now Fort Liberty). In 1927, Pinehurst hosted seven teams who vied for the trophy. Teams from Harvard, Yale, Princeton, and Fort Bragg competed. Army won the battle.

American humorist Will Rogers frequently came to Pinehurst to play polo. Unlike the other players, Rogers refused to wear jodhpurs, boots, and a polo helmet, preferring his street clothes and fedora instead. Slocock said Rogers was a good player but that he "likes to clown through the game." Go figure. Rogers would sometimes play polo during the day and then head to the Pinehurst Theatre to perform at night.

Lawn Bowling

The answer is not much if you're wondering about the difference between lawn bowling and bocce. Both are strategic, skills-based games involving

Lawn bowls at Pinehurst Country Club. *Moore County Historical Association.*

rolling balls on a grass surface with the intent of hitting targets. The difference is in the details. Bocce balls are round, while those for lawn bowling are elliptical. Players toss the ball in bocce, while those for lawn bowling roll the ball. The court surface and size differ, and so does their origin. Lawn bowling (or "lawn bowls," as villagers call it) originates in England, whereas the much older bocce dates back to ancient Rome. If you drive up to the Pinehurst Country Club and see a team of players dressed in whites bowling on a small green, there's a good chance it's a national or international competition in lawn bowls. Pinehurst remains a popular destination for the sport.

KNOLLWOOD AIRPORT

On November 11, 1931, a thin woman landed at Knollwood Airport (now Moore County Airport) and greeted the manager, Lloyd O. Yost, along with a hundred or so spectators who had gathered. Folks had turned out to see the famous aviator Amelia Earhart, who had touched down to refuel after a busy day of festivities in Fayetteville. Earhart told a local reporter she was "pleased to spot the word 'PINEHURST' displayed in giant letters on the roof of Knollwood Field's hanger." Earhart stayed about twenty-five

Amelia Earhart at Knollwood Airport. *Tufts Archives.*

minutes, long enough to refuel and shake a few hands. Then she was off. A few years later, Earhart and her husband, George Putnam, were back as guests, staying at the Carolina Hotel for a week of rest. According to a society reporter, their stay "was presumably coupled with a visit to George's mother who had taken the Schaumberg House on New York Avenue in Southern Pines for the season."

In 1929, Earhart and five other female pilots founded the 99 Club, a group of flyers who promoted women in aviation. Earhart was the organization's first president, and a few Pinehurst residents were early members: Mrs. W.D. Hyatt and Mrs. Richard Clemson, who both joined in 1937.

Mr. and Mrs. Clemson, both licensed pilots, wintered in Mid Pines. Mrs. Clemson (the *Outlook* never gives her first name) was a championship golfer, beating Myra Paterson for the 1927 St. Valentine's trophy. She was an avid tennis player, philanthropist, and society maven, fond of afternoon teas and bridge games. She said the Southeast division of the 99 Club, which includes the Sandhills, was "extremely active." Newspaper accounts from the time corroborate that Knollwood Airport was especially active with women flyers.

The Clemsons owned a private airport, Star Haven, in Middletown, New York, where Mrs. C. sometimes sponsored air meets for fellow members of the 99 Club. According to Clemson, the meet gave the women a chance to "get together for aeronautical chats, to go aloft together, to get better acquainted." She describes the club as a "group of aviatrixes chiefly interested in the promotion of the science of flying." Clemson flew a high-winged monoplane, which she dubbed "Madame Queen IV." Like many pilots, she preferred to fly than drive, no longer feeling safe in a car. She describes flying in lyrical terms: "Nothing will make you more humble than flying. Not at first, of course, because then you are so pleased to have conquered an element that you feel that you have the world by the tail. But the more you fly, the more you change."

BIBLIOGRAPHY

Chapter 1: Pinehurst, 1 B.G. (Before Golf)

"About Edward Everett Hale." Lend a Hand Society. 2020. lend-a-hand-society.org/about.

"About LAH." Lend a Hand Society. 2020. lend-a-hand-society.org/about.

Baldwin, Brooke. "The Cakewalk: A Study in Stereotype and Reality." *Journal of Social History* 15, no. 2 (1981): 205–18. www.jstor.org/stable/3787107.

Britannica, T. Editors of Encyclopedia. "Edward Everett Hale." *Encyclopedia Britannica*, June 6, 2023. www.britannica.com/biography/Edward-Everett-Hale.

Buie, Chris. *The Early Days of Pinehurst*. N.p., 2014.

"The Casino Building: A Pinehurst Landmark." Pinehurst Properties Inc. 1989.

Gray, Ethel M., to Leonard Tufts. July 18, 1919. Tufts Archives [hereafter TA].

Grey, Ethel. "A History of Pinehurst." *Pinehurst Outlook*, January 23, 1932, 4.

"A Guide to the Historic Village of Pinehurst, North Carolina: A National Historic Landmark." TA. 2017.

Harlow, Robert E. "Pinehurst History." *Pinehurst Outlook*, November 4, 1945, 1, 5.

Himel, Matthew Taylor. "Greening Golf: Grass, Agriculture and Pinehurst in the Sandhills." PhD diss., Mississippi State University, 2020.

"His Influence on Pinehurst's Future Was Great." *Pinehurst Outlook*, January 19, 1938, 6, 13.

Koch, Lou. "Out of Bounds." *Pinehurst Outlook*, January 16, 1937, 17.

Moriarty, Audrey. *Pinehurst: Golf, History, and the Good Life*. Ann Arbor, MI: Sports Media Group, 2005.

Moss, Richard J. *Eden in the Pines: A History of Pinehurst Village*. Southern Pines, NC: The Pilot, 2005.

North, Raymond E. *The Pinehurst Story: June 1895–June 1984*. Pinehurst, NC: Resorts of Pinehurst, 1984.

"Our Trees and Shrubs." *Pinehurst Outlook*, November 5, 1897, 1.

Owens, Ray. "Adam of Our Eden." *Pinehurst Living*, n.d., 65–69.

Pinehurst and the Village Chapel. Pinehurst, NC: Pinehurst Religious Association, 1957.

Powell, William S., ed. "James Walker Tufts." *Dictionary of North Carolina Biography*. Chapel Hill: University of North Carolina Press, 1979–96.

"Protege, Planner, Planter." *Mass Golfer* (Fall 2007): 17.

Schlosser, Jim. "Who's Manning? Pinehurst Designer Unsung." *News and Record*, June 18, 2005, A7.

Shrum, Regan. "Who Takes the Cake?" National Museum of American History, blog post, May 18, 2016.

Tufts, James Walker, to physicians. November 22, 1895. TA.

Tufts, Richard S. "The First Seventy-Five Years: A History of the Village of Pinehurst." Unpublished manuscript, n.d., TA.

Village of Pinehurst: A Walking Tour. Pinehurst, NC: Convention and Visitors Bureau, 2009.

Watt, William H. "A Brief History of Pinehurst." *Pinehurst Outlook*, March 1944.

Youngs, Larry R. "Creating America's Winter Golfing Mecca at Pinehurst, North Carolina: National Marketing and Local Control." *Journal of Sport History*, 30, no. 1 (2003): 25–41.

Chapter 2: The Caddies

Batten, Sammy. "Pinehurst Honors Caddies." *Fayetteville Observer*, n.d.

Bergmann, Charlie. "In the Loop: Willie McRae Joining Caddie Hall of Fame." *The Pilot*, October 19, 2003, B1.

"Black History in Golf, a Story." African American Registry, April 8, 2008. www.aaregistry.org.

Butler, Bion. "Recollections: Our Colored Friends." *Pinehurst Outlook*, March 14, 1931, 11.

Cadieu, Beth. "In the Middle of Golf Stream." *Pinehurst Outlook*, October 14, 1976, 2.

Case, Bill. "It Takes a Village."*PineStraw Magazine*, June 27, 2023.

Criswell, Stephen. "Dr. Buzzard." South Carolina Encyclopedia. www.scencyclopedia.org/sce/entries/dr-buzzard.

Davis, Jim. "The Caddy Experience at Pinehurst." Golf Heritage Society. 2020. www.golfheritage.org.

Demas, Lane. *Game of Privilege: An African American History of Golf*. Chapel Hill: University of North Carolina Press, 2017.

deNissoff, Mary Evelyn. "Pinehurst from Its Birth According to 'Hardrock.'" *The Pilot*, December 29, 1994.

Dunn, Paul. "It's Time to Honor the Caddies of Pinehurst." *The Pilot*, February 21, 2016, B3.

Embrey, Tom. "It's a Family Affair: McRaes Are Special Part of Pinehurst Golf Legacy." *The Pilot*, June 15, 2014.

Gandhi, Lakshmi. "The Extraordinary Story of Why a 'Cakewalk' Wasn't Always Easy." NPR, December 23, 2013.

"Hardrock—The Rock a Fixture at Pinehurst." *Pinehurst Gazette*, n.d., 14.

Himel, Matthew Taylor. "Greening Golf: Grass, Agriculture, and Pinehurst in the Sandhills." PhD diss., Mississippi State University, 2020.

"Horse Chatter." *Pinehurst Outlook*, February 12, 1938, 16.

In Memory of Robert "Hardrock" Robinson. Pamphlet, March 10, 2002.

"An Interview About Caddies." *Pinehurst Outlook*, January 7, 1933.

Jordan, Gunby G. *Caddies*. Columbus, GA: Green Island Press, 1987.

McDonald, Pete. *Uneven Lies: The Heroic Story of African-Americans in Golf*. Greenwich, CT: American Golfer, 2000.

McRae Willie. *On the Bag: Seventy Years Remembered by Pinehurst's Hall-of-Fame Caddie*. Cincinnati, OH: Stevens Publishing, 2013.

Moriarty, Audrey. *Pinehurst: Golf, History, and the Good Life*. Ann Arbor, MI: Sports Media Group, 2005.

O'Brien, Kathy. "Tom Cotton Picturesque Character." World Golf Hall of Fame Tournament Program, PGA Seniors, 1983.

Ormsy, Ed. "Goodbye: Lost Ball Brings Back Memories of 'Hard Rock.'" *The Pilot*, November 12, 2006.

Pace, Lee. "The Soul of a Caddie." *PineStraw Magazine*, March 2012, 52–53.

Pinehurst Inc. to Donald Ross, January 19, 1924. TA.

Pinehurst Inc. to Judge George H. Humber, June 27, 1927. TA.

Pinehurst Inc. to Lucile Eiford, February 19, 1925. TA.

Ross, Alan. "Golf's His Game." *American Profile*, n.d., 12.

Ross, Helen. "Gaines Is a Pinehurst Institution: A Legend of the Links Still Carries On." *Greensboro News and Record*, January 25, 2015.

Saunders, Barry. "A Caddie's Love of the Game." *The Pilot*, June 17, 2014.

Schlosser, Jim. "Black Town Outgrows Role at Pinehurst." *Greensboro News and Record*, January 19, 1990.

Sinclair, David. "Pinehurst Resort Loses a Legend." *The Pilot*, October 31, 2018.

Tomlinson, Tommy. "Pinehurst Greens Reader." *Our State*, January 2015, 130–34.

Ward, Howard. "Caddies for the Ages: Pinehurst Honors Its Most Famous Bag Carriers." *The Pilot*, April 11, 2001, B5.

Wiles, Laurie Bogart. "Brothers Under the Skin." *Golf Sports Magazine*, June/July 2014, 76–84.

Chapter 3: The Sandhills Woman's Exchange

"An Early Pictorial History of the Sandhills Woman's Exchange: 2022 Calendar." Southern Pines, NC: Whistle Stop Press, 2022.

"Exchange Makes Plans for Opening on October 3." *The Pilot*, September 21, 1977, 34.

"Federation of Woman's Exchanges." *WEFED*, December 1, 2022.

"Helping Others to Help Themselves Is the Theme of the Sandhills Woman's Exchange." *Citizen News and Record*, May 28, 1986, 4.

Hill, Kermit. "This Old Cabin." *Moore County Source*, October 1984.

Kelly, Susan Stafford. "The Sandhill's Woman's Exchange." *Our State*, February 28, 2022.

Madeley, Claudia. "Sandhills Woman's Exchange Reopens Sept 16 for Season." *Sandhill Citizen and News Outlook*, September 7, 1985.

Pilgrim, David. "The Mammy Caricature." Jim Crow Museum, Ferris State University. October 2000.

Salomon, Deborah. "Cabin Fever." *Pinestraw Magazine*, January 2021.

Sandhills Woman's Exchange Meeting Minutes. TA. May 8, 1923; November 5, 1923; December 12, 1923; January 16, 1924; April 9, 1924; April 23, 1924; June 1924; November 21, 1924; December 3, 1924; January 7, 1925; February 9, 1927; March 9, 1927; December 8, 1927; April 17, 1930; March 13, 1931; April 22, 1931; April 25, 1931; November 25,

1932; February 6, 1933; April 19, 1933; February 16, 1940; January 10, 1941; February 14, 1941; March 14, 1941; November 15, 1941; February 13, 1942; November 13, 1942; April 9, 1943; December 10, 1943; January 12, 1945; December 7, 1945; April 9, 1948; February 1950; February 8, 1965; February 14, 1977; March 10, 1977.

"Sandhills Woman's Exchange Opens." *Charlotte Observer*, February 9, 1962.

Walker, Jean Barron. "The Sandhills Woman's Exchange." *Pinehurst Living Magazine*, n.d., 57–60.

Chapter 4: Annie Oakley

"Annie Oakley Gives an Exhibition." *Pinehurst Outlook*, March 17, 1920, 4.

Burba, Howard. "From Circus Fame to Lace and Silver Hair: Annie Oakley's Advice to Women." *Dayton Daily News Magazine and Fiction Section*, May 16, 1926.

Carney, Peter P. "Greatest of Modern Diana's." *Pinehurst Outlook*, March 17, 1921, 1.

Cox, Clark. "AO's Visits to Pinehurst Were Legendary." *The Pilot*, May 4, 2003, D5.

"Doings in Real Estate." *Pinehurst Outlook*, December 15, 1923, 5.

Garner, Margie. "Film Stirs Memories of Annie Oakley and Frank Butler at Pinehurst Club." *The Pilot*, April 18, 1950, 8.

Hines, Michele. "Little Sure Shot." *Ashboro Courier-Tribune*, May 23, 1999.

Kasper, Shirl. *Annie Oakley*. Norman: University of Oklahoma Press, 1992.

———. "Annie Oakley: The Magical Year in London." *Montana: The Magazine of Western History* 42, no. 2 (1992): 22–37.

"Little Horn Comes Back." *Pinehurst Outlook*, March 10, 1917, 1.

McClellan, Barbara. "A Crusade for Annie Oakley, the Lady." *Detroit News*, February 4, 1987, 8D.

"The Minstrels Evening of Music and Fun." *Sandhill Citizen*, February 18, 1921, 1.

"Minstrel Show and Vaudeville." *Sandhill Citizen*, February 18, 1921, 2.

Moeser, Helen. "The Pinehurst Gun Club and the Annie Oakley Connection." *Pinehurst Magazine*, November/December 1991, 18–23.

Moriarty, Matthews. "Annie in the Pines." *PineStraw Magazine*, June 2009.

"Powder and Pigeons." *Pinehurst Outlook*, November 1, 1919, 17.

"Promising Pupils of Annie Oakley Blaze Away at the Gun Club." *Pinehurst Outlook*, January 14, 1920, 1.

Righthand, Jess. "How Annie Oakley, 'Princess of the West,' Preserved Her Ladylike Reputation." *Smithsonian Magazine*, April 11, 2010.

Riley, Glenda. *The Life and Legacy of Annie Oakley*. Norman: University of Oklahoma Press, 1994.

Saunders, Trudy Haywood. "When Annie Oakley Came to Pinehurst." *Garden and Gun Magazine*, March 16, 2021.

Sayers, Isabelle S. *Annie Oakley and Buffalo Bill's Wild West*. Dover, NY, 1981.

"Society Circus; Sandhills Grooming Its Talent to Emulate Barnum." *Pinehurst Outlook*, February 9, 1918, 11.

Vonada, Damaine. "Annie Oakley Was More Than a 'Crack Shot in Petticoats.'" *Smithsonian Magazine*, September 1990, 131–47.

Walker, Carol. "The Rest Is History: Annie Oakley at Pinehurst." *The Clay Pigeon*, February 1999.

Walker, Jean Barron. "Annie Oakley in Pinehurst." *Pinehurst Living Magazine*, n.d., 48–51.

Wills, Chuck. *Annie Oakley: A Photographic Story of a Life*. New York: DK Publishing, 2007.

Chapter 5: The Women's North and South

Case, Bill. "The Natural." *PineStraw Magazine*, February 2019.

"Champions Defeated: North and South Golf Tournament Develops Some Surprises." *Pinehurst Outlook*, March 30, 1918, 1–2.

Dreyspool, Joan Flynn. "The Lady." *Golf Graphic*, 1954, 4–9.

Emory, Pamela F. "Heroes of American Golf: Glenna Collett Vare." *Links* (Summer n.d.): 32–36.

"Estelle Lawson Page, by Magnificent Performance, Wins National Golf Title." *Chapel Hill Weekly*, October 15, 1937, 1.

Eubanks, Steve. "Women's Golf's Greatest Forgotten Champion." LPGA. com, March 17, 2021.

"Glenna Sports Women's Golfing Crown for the Third Time This Season." *Pinehurst Outlook*, November 1928, 14.

Glenn, Rhonda. *The Illustrated History of Women's Golf*. Dallas: Taylor Publishing, 1991.

Goodner, Ross. "Glenna Collett." *Golf's Greatest: The Legendary World Golf Hall of Famers*, 33–39.

Harlow, Robert E. "Estelle Lawson Page, Housewife and Champion Golfer." *Pinehurst Outlook*, February 5, 1938, 7–8.

Hartman, Robert. *Tales from Pinehurst: Stories from the Mecca of American Golf.* New York: Sports Publishing, 2004.

Jones, Joe. "Lawson Golf Course." *Chapel Hill Weekly*, n.d., 1, 8.

"Longtime Top Amateur Peggy Kirk Bell, a Proponent for Women's Golf, Dies at 95." ESPN, Associated Press. November 24, 2016.

Macdonald, Robert S., and Herbert Warren Wind, eds. *The Great Women Golfers.* New York: Ailsa Publishing, 1994.

McNiblick, Sandy. "Mrs. Barlow Comes to Pinehurst Again." *Pinehurst Outlook,* January 14, 1920, 7.

"Mrs. Barlow Champion." *Pinehurst Outlook*, April 1, 1916.

"North and South Championship." *Pinehurst Outlook*, March 31, 1921.

Pace, Bill. *The Spirit of Pinehurst.* Pinehurst, NC: Pinehurst Inc., 2004.

Pace, Lee. *Pinehurst Stories: A Celebration of Great Golf and Good Times.* Pinehurst, NC: Resorts of Pinehurst, 1991.

"Sergeant Julian Page Severely Wounded in Action on the Continent." *Pinehurst Outlook*, April 20, 1945, 5.

Twiss, Jack. "Mrs. J.V. Hurd Regains North and South Title." *Pinehurst Outlook*, n.d., 4, 9.

"U.S. Women's Amateur." *The Official Golf Guide.* 1948. TA.

White, Gordon. "Impressive Lady: Orcutt Combined Passion for Golf, Writing." *The Pilot,* January 12, 2007, 1, 4.

Wilson, Enid. "Mid-Century Musings." *Golf World Magazine*, n.d.

Wind, Herbert Warren. *The Story of American Golf*. Vol. 1. New York: Callaway Editions, 1948.

Youngs, Larry R. "Creating America's Winter Golfing Mecca at Pinehurst, North Carolina: National Marketing and Local Control." *Journal of Sports History* (Spring 2003): 25–41.

Chapter 6: Jalopy Soccer and Pig Races

"The Archers Company Fine Bows and Arrows" (brochure), 1931.

"Archery at Resorts." *Pinehurst Outlook*, February 13, 1909, 5.

"Archery-Golf." *Pinehurst Outlook,* January 21, 1933, 12.

"Archery: The Sport of Romance and Tradition" (brochure), 1932.

Bond, Constance. "We Couldn't Stop Playing to Save Our Souls." *Smithsonian Magazine*, June 1987, 120–22.

"Bows and Arrows." *Pinehurst Outlook,* January 31, 1931, 11.

Boznos, Chris. "The Origin of Miniature Golf and 'Thistle Dhu.'" NCPEDIA, 2012.

Douma, Michael J. "A Brief History of the Origins of Croquet in America." *Creative Historical Thinking*, January 3, 2022.

"Early American Pageant Features Races." *Pinehurst Outlook*, March 1, 1929, 5.

Eberle, Ann. "Croquet and Lawn Bowls: A Pinehurst Tradition." N.d., 30–31, 44.

"Equestrian Gymkhanas Entertain Participants and Onlookers." *Pinehurst Outlook*, December 2, 1905, 3.

Frost, Natasha. "The Ninety-Nines Was Amelia Earhart's Club for Female Aviators." Atlas Obscura, June 6, 2018. www.atlasobscura.com/articles/female-aviators-ninety-nines-amelia-earhart.

"The Giant Bows of Old Japan." *Pinehurst Outlook*, March 8, 1930, 6.

"Golf Course Changes." *Pinehurst Outlook*, November 28, 1903, 5.

"Great Tennis." *Pinehurst Outlook*, April 12, 1919, 1.

"Gymkhanas, Paper Chases and Saddle Picnics Add to Interest." *Pinehurst Outlook*, December 1906, 10.

"Introducing a New Sport—Archery." *Pinehurst Outlook*, November 1, 1926, 6.

"Kiwanis Club: Philip Rounsevelle Tells Kiwanians Secrets of Making Bows and Arrows." *Sandhill Citizen*, August 6, 1926, 1.

Koch, L.A. "Sports Review: Early Spring Heralds a Busy Season." *Pinehurst Outlook*, February 29, 1936.

Koch, Lou. "Man About Town." *Pinehurst Outlook*, January 6, 1940, 3.

"The Magic Word Gymkhana." *Pinehurst Outlook*, December 9, 1911, 7.

"Mrs. Rounsevelle Leads Archery." *Pinehurst* Outlook, January 18, 1929, 5.

"Noted Jumping Pony Due at Gymkhana." *Pinehurst Outlook*, February 4, 1940, 1.

"Notes from the Firing Line." *Pinehurst Outlook*, January 11, 1929, 5.

"Out of Bounds." *Pinehurst Outlook*, December 8, 1934, 4.

"Out of Bounds." *Pinehurst Outlook*, March 9, 1935, 2.

Pace, Lee. "The Art of Lilliputian Golf: 'Thistle Dhu' Hails from a Storied Tradition." *The Pilot*, June 19, 2014.

"Pinehurst Hotel Notes." *Pinehurst Outlook*, April 12, 1927, 10.

"Pinehurst's Headquarters for Archery" (ad), n.d.

"Range, Tee and Track." *Pinehurst Outlook*, February 1929, 6.

"Sandhills Polo Club Makes Its Bow." *Pinehurst Outlook*, February 11, 1920.

Scott, Richard Lee. "Lloyd O. Yost, Pilot." *Pinehurst Outlook*, March 11, 1933, 5.

Seiwell, Don T. "Winston-Sale Poloists Carry Off Honors in Seventh Annual Tilt." *Pinehurst Outlook*, December 21, 1928.

"Social News of the Pinehurst Week." *Pinehurst Outlook*, March 4, 1933, 1.

"Social Notes of the Week." *Pinehurst Outlook*, January 25, 1929, 6.

"Social Notes of the Week." *Pinehurst Outlook*, April 12, 1929, 9.

Stern, F.A. "Pen Portrait in Blue Ink: One Ninety Niner." *Pinehurst Outlook*, February 25, 1939, 7.

"Tennis Holds the Spotlight." *Pinehurst Outlook*, April 23, 1938, 7.

"Turkey-Driving Event to Feature Gymkhana Program." *Pinehurst Outlook*, November 29, 1939, 2.

Walker, Jean Barron. "Thistle Dhu: Then and Now." *Pinehurst Living*, September/October 2016, 48–51.

Wiles, Laurie Bogart. "Finding Mr. Barber: The Mystery of the Most Influential Man in the Sandhills." *PineStraw Magazine*, February 2015, 60–64.

Wisell, Edward H. "The Golf Course at Thistle Dhu." *Popular Science Magazine* 95, no. 2 (1919): 84–86.

ABOUT THE AUTHOR

Julia Hans, PhD, is a national award-winning essayist who writes about American history and culture. She graduated from the University of Massachusetts–Amherst in 2011 with a doctorate in American literature. Formerly, Hans worked as a journalist, writing profiles and features for various Massachusetts newspapers. Local history was part of the beat. A New England transplant, Hans moved to North Carolina to escape the winters and be near family. She started archival research about Pinehurst to prepare for a gig as a history tour guide, which led to this book. Find her work at www.juliahans.com.